PBS LiteracyLink®
Workplace Essential Skills

READING

by Bernice Golden

PBS LiteracyLink®

KET
The Kentucky
Network

NCAL

LiteracyLink is a joint project of the PBS, Kentucky Educational Television, the National
Center on Adult Literacy, and the Kentucky Department of Education. This project is funded
in whole, or in part, by the Star Schools Program of the USDE under contract #R203D60001.

Acknowledgments

LiteracyLink® Advisory Board

Dr. Drew Albritton, American Association for
  Adult and Continuing Education
Peggy Barber, American Library Association
Anthony Buttino, WNED-TV
Dr. Anthony Carnevale, Educational Testing Service
Dr. Patricia Edwards, Michigan State University
Maggi Gaines, Baltimore Reads, Inc.
Dr. Milton Goldberg, National Alliance for Business
Columbus Hartwell, Exodus
Jan Hawkins, Center for Children and Technology,
  Education Development Corporation, Inc.
Neal Johnson, Educational Testing Service
Dr. Cynthia Johnston, Central Piedmont
  Community College
Thomas Kinney, American Association of Adult
  and Continuing Education
Dr. Jacqueline E. Korengel, Kentucky Department
  for Adult Ed and Literacy
Michael O'Brian, Certain Teed Corporation
Rafael Ramirez, U.S. Deptartment of Education
Dr. Emma Rhodes, Formerly of Arkansas Department
  of Education
Dr. Ahmed Sabie, Kentucky Department of Adult
  Education and Literacy
Tony Sarmiento, Worker Centered Learning,
  Working for America Institute
Dr. Steve Steurer, Correctional Education Association
Dr. Alice Tracy, Correctional Education Association
Dr. Fran Tracy-Mumford, Delaware Department of
  Adult/Community Education
Dr. Terilyn Turner, Community Education, St. Paul
  Public Schools
Dr. Renee Westcott, Central Piedmont Community
  College

Ex Officio Advisory Members

Joan Aucher, GED Testing Service
Cheryl Garnette, U.S. Department of Education
Dr. Andrew Hartman, National Institute for Literacy
Dr. Mary Lovell, U.S. Department of Education
Ronald Pugsley, U.S. Department of Education
Dr. Linda Roberts, U.S. Department of Education
Joe Wilkes, U.S. Department of Education

LiteracyLink Partners

LiteracyLink is a joint project of the Public Broadcasting
Service, Kentucky Educational Television, the National
Center on Adult Literacy, and the Kentucky Department
of Education. This project is funded in whole, or in part,
by the Star Schools Program of the USDE under contract
#R203D60001.

Special thanks to the Kentucky Department for
Adult Education and Literacy, Workforce Development
Cabinet for its help on this project and for its vision and
commitment to excellence in helping provide superior
adult education products and services.

Workbook Production

Developer:
Learning Unlimited, Oak Park, Illinois

Design:
PiperStudios Inc., Chicago, Illinois

Cover Design and Layout:
By Design, Lexington, Kentucky

Project Consultant:
Milli Fazey, KET, Lexington, Kentucky

Production Manager:
Margaret Norman, KET, Lexington, Kentucky

ISBN 1-881020-36-3
ISBN 1-978-1-881020-36-3

Table of Contents

To the Teacher

The purpose of the *Workplace Essential Skills* series is to enable adult learners to become better informed and more highly skilled for the changing world of work. The materials are aimed at adults who are at the pre-GED (6th- to 8th-grade) reading level.

Twenty-four *Workplace Essential Skills* **television programs** model the application of basic skills within the context of pre-employment and workplace settings. The four accompanying **workbooks** present instruction, practice, and application of the critical skills that are represented in the programs:

- *Employment*
- *Communication & Writing*
- *Reading*
- *Mathematics*

The series includes a utilization program for instructors and an overview program for learners.

The series also includes a **teacher's guide** for instructors and an **assessment instrument** to help learners and instructors determine the most effective course of study in the *Workplace Essential Skills* series.

Each lesson in the *Reading* workbook corresponds to one of the four reading television programs in the *Workplace Essential Skills* series. The topics in the *Reading* workbook and the video programs are based on common labor market and workplace tasks.

Basic skills, problem solving, and decision making are integrated into every lesson. Additionally, interdisciplinary connections are inserted throughout the books for practice in real-world reading, writing, communication, math, and technology skills.

Taken together, the features and components of the *Workplace Essential Skills* instructional program provide a comprehensive grounding in the knowledge and skills learners need to succeed in the world of work. By also utilizing the ***LiteracyLink*** on-line component (see page vii), learners will begin to develop some of the computer literacy and Internet know-how needed to advance in the workplace of today and tomorrow.

Many of the skills covered in *Workplace Essential Skills* also provide a foundation for GED-level work in the areas of reading, math, and writing. Because high school completion is an important prerequisite for advancement in the work world, learners should be encouraged to go on to GED-level study when they are ready to do so. The ***LiteracyLink*** GED videos, print, and on-line materials (available in the year 2000) will provide an ideal context for learners to prepare for the GED tests and fulfill the requirement of high school equivalency.

To the Learner

Welcome to *Workplace Essential Skills: Reading*. This workbook has been designed to help you learn more about the ideas and skills presented in Programs 16–19 of the *Workplace Essential Skills* series. Take time to read about some of the features in this book.

1. The **Skills Preview** on pages 1–11 will help you discover which video programs and workbook lessons are most important for you. You can use the **Skills Preview Evaluation Chart** on page 11 to make your own personal study plan.

2. Each workbook lesson goes with a program in the television series. The lessons in this workbook cover Programs 16–19. Use the program number and title to find the corresponding tape and workbook lesson. After the opening page and **Objectives,** each lesson is divided into two parts:

    Before You Watch starts you thinking about the topics in the video program.

    - **Sneak Preview:** Exercise to preview some of the key concepts from the program.
    - **Answers for Sneak Preview:** Answers to the preview exercise.
    - **Feedback:** Information to help you personalize your work.
    - **Vocabulary:** Key terms from the lesson and their definitions.

    After You Watch allows you to apply skills that you saw in the program.

    - **Key Points from the Video Program:** List that summarizes the program.
    - **Situations:** Real-world problem solving from the health care, manufacturing, service, retail, and construction industries.
    - **Information:** In-depth information about important workplace concepts.
    - **WorkTips:** Hints for success in the world of work.
    - **WorkSkills:** Exercise that enables you to apply what you have learned.
    - **Connections:** Extension of workplace skills through practice in other content areas. (*Write It, Tech Tip, Read It, Math Matters,* and *Communicate*)
    - **Review:** Section that lets you put all of your new workplace knowledge together.

3. The **Skills Review** allows you to evaluate what you have learned.

4. The **Answer Key** starts on page 105. There you can find answers to the exercises in each lesson, often with explanations, as well as samples of filled-in forms and documents.

5. The **Glossary,** which starts on page 112, includes key terms and definitions.

6. You can use the alphabetized **Index,** which starts on page 114, to look up information about reading issues.

7. A **Reference Handbook,** found on pages 117–132, is a helpful resource for you to access at any time. References to the handbook are listed throughout the book.

Instructional Units

Units of study are used to organize *LiteracyLink's* instruction. For example, the first unit in this book is Reading for a Purpose. To study this topic, you can use a video, workbook lesson, and computer. You will be able to easily find what you need since each workbook unit has the same title as a video and related Internet activities.

Getting Started With the System

It is possible to use each *LiteracyLink* component separately. However, you will make the best use of *LiteracyLink* if you use all of the parts. You can make this work in a way that is best for you through the *LiteracyLink* Internet site.

On the Internet site, you will take a Welcome Tour and establish your Home Space. The Home Space is your starting point for working through the online portion of *LiteracyLink*. It is also a place where you can save all of your online work.

An important part of the online system is LitHelper℠. This helps you to identify your strengths and weaknesses. LitHelper℠ helps you to develop an individualized study plan. The online LitLearner® materials, together with the videos and workbooks, provide hundreds of learning opportunities. Go to http://www.pbs.org/literacy to access the online material.

For Teachers

Parts of *LiteracyLink* have been developed for adult educators and service providers. LitTeacher® is an online professional development system. It provides a number of resources including PeerLit℠ a database of evaluated websites. At http://www.pbs.org/literacy you can also access *LitTeacher*.

Who's Responsible for *LiteracyLink*?

LiteracyLink was sparked by a five-year grant by the U.S. Department of Education. The following partners have contributed to the development of the *LiteracyLink* system:
- PBS Adult Learning Service
- Kentucky Educational Television (KET)
- The National Center on Adult Literacy (NCAL) of the University of Pennsylvania
- The Kentucky Department of Education

The *LiteracyLink* partners wish you the very best in achieving your educational goals.

The LiteracyLink® System

Welcome to the *LiteracyLink* system. This workbook is one part of an educational system for adult learners and adult educators.

LiteracyLink consists of these learning tools:

Television programs
broadcast on
public television
and in adult
learning centers

Computer-based materials
available
through a
connection to the Internet

Workbooks
print-based
instruction
and practice

If you are working with *LiteracyLink* materials, you have a clear educational advantage. As you develop your knowledge and skills, you are also working with video and computer technology. This is the technology required to succeed in today's workplace, training programs, and colleges.

Content of the *LiteracyLink* System

The *LiteracyLink* system allows you to choose what you need to meet your goals. It consists of instruction and practice in the areas of:

Workplace Essential Skills
- Employment
  Pre-Employment and On-the-Job Skills
- Communication & Writing
  Listening, Speaking, and Writing Skills
- Reading
  Charts, Forms, Documents, and Manuals
- Mathematics
  Whole Numbers, Decimals, Fractions, and Percents

GED Preparation Series
- Language Arts Reading
  Fiction, Nonfiction, Poetry, Drama and Informational
- Language Arts Writing
  Essay Writing, Sentence Structure, Grammar, and Mechanics
- Social Studies
  U.S. History, World History, Geography, Civics and Government, and Economics
- Science
  Life Sciences, Earth and Space Sciences, Chemistry, and Physics
- Mathematics
  Arithmetic, Data Analysis, Algebra, and Geometry

Skills Preview

On the following pages is a Skills Preview. This preview will help you find out how well you can read and use workplace reading materials.

On the preview, you will see the kind of real-life materials that workers need to read in order to do their jobs. These reading materials include memos, forms, charts, instructions, and manuals. After each reading is a set of questions. They ask you to show how well you understood the reading and to use the information as a worker would on the job. The questions may be multiple choice or short answer.

Read each piece of workplace material carefully and then answer the questions based on it. For a multiple-choice question, circle the number of the answer you have chosen. For a short-answer question, write on the line provided. Feel free to go back and reread to find the answer to a question if you want to.

When you are finished taking the Skills Preview, you can check your answers and complete the evaluation chart. In this way, you will be able to see what reading skills you do well and what skills you need to work on. Then you can focus on those skills as you work through the four reading programs: Reading for a Purpose, Finding What You Need: Forms and Charts, Following Directions, and Reading Reports and Manuals. Each program has both a video and a section of lessons in this workbook.

After you have watched all the videos and completed the workbook lessons, you can take a Skills Review. Save your responses to this preview and compare them with your results on the review. Then you will see how much you have learned.

Questions 1–4 are based on the following situation.

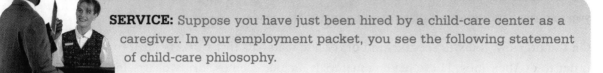

SERVICE: Suppose you have just been hired by a child-care center as a caregiver. In your employment packet, you see the following statement of child-care philosophy.

Philosophy at Kids' Corner
Kids' Corner has a child-centered philosophy:

Each child is unique. Each child has his or her own needs that must be met and abilities that must be developed. We provide for a child's total development—physical, cognitive, social, and emotional.

A child best develops physically in a safe and healthful environment. We provide sound nutrition and hygiene and protected indoor and outdoor play.

A child best develops cognitively by exploring and doing. We promote and challenge each child's understanding with age-appropriate materials and activities.

A child best develops socially and emotionally through close, warm relationships with other people. We are always available and responsive to each child. We respect each child. And we foster responsive and respectful relationships among the children in our care.

---

1. What is the main purpose of this statement?

   (1) to train you in child care
   (2) to inform you how children at the center are treated
   (3) to explain childhood development
   (4) to direct you to do specific job tasks

2. What is the overall main idea of the statement?

   (1) Each child at Kids' Corner is unique.
   (2) All children at Kids' Corner develop their abilities.
   (3) The Kids' Corner program centers on children's needs.
   (4) Kids' Corner is a safe place to leave a child.

3. When the statement discusses cognitive development, it is referring to how a child

   (1) thinks and learns
   (2) plays and works
   (3) sees and hears
   (4) jumps and runs

4. An example of fostering "responsive and respectful relationships among children" would be a caregiver trying to get a child to

(1) eat   (3) obey

(2) sleep   (4) share

Questions 5–9 are based on the following chart.

You are assigned as an aide to the 2-year-olds' room at the child-care center. The chart shown below is on the wall of the room.

NAME	CUBBY	COAT HANGER	COT
Alverez, Maria	1	1	1
Benito, Juan	2	2	2
Brown, Mel	3	3	3
~~Dorwin, Nan~~	~~4~~	~~4~~	~~4~~
Fisher, Ann	5	5	5
* Gray, Lisa	6	6	6
Lotoya, Jim	7	7	7
Uzman, Tariq	8	8	8
** White, Jasmine	6	6	6
Jones, Tomi	9	9	9
Spellman, Erin	4	4	4

* Attends mornings only   ** Attends afternoons only

5. The purpose of the chart is to

(1) record children's attendance

(2) note children's cubby, coat hanger, and cot assignments

(3) outline activities for each child

(4) give a daily schedule

6. Who uses cubby 2?

(1) Maria   (3) Mel

(2) Juan   (4) Nan

7. Explain why Lisa and Jasmine can share the same hanger and cot.

_____

8. Why do you think there is a line through Nan Dorwin's name?

_____

9. What happened to Nan Dorwin's assignments?

_____

Questions 10–13 are based on the following situation.

WORK ORDER		
Job Location J. Framer 341 Woodview Drive Springfield, KY **Phone No.** 555-1929	**Job No.** 143 **Materials** SealMate Shingles 15 lb. felt 30 lb. felt ice and water shield	**Report Date** July 5

JOB TASKS
Complete tear off of roofing material. Inspect roof boards and renail if needed. Install 15 lb. felt paper and heavy SealMate shingles. Rework all flashings into roof. Replace old roof vents with new ones. Install ice and water shield at bottom of all valleys. Install 30 lb. felt paper down center of all valleys. Paint existing soil stacks to match color of roof. Clean and haul away old debris. _____   _____ Crew head signature   Date of completion

10. The purpose of this form is to

    (1) detail the tasks for putting a new roof on a house
    (2) explain how to put a roof on a house
    (3) order materials needed to put a roof on a house
    (4) evaluate a roofing job done on a house

11. Whose house is getting a new roof?

    _____

12. When should the job start?

    _____

13. Who must sign the form?

    (1) the owner of the house
    (2) the owner of the roofing company
    (3) the purchaser of the roofing materials
    (4) the head of the work crew

Questions 14–18 are based on the following chart.

SealMate Shingles		
COLOR	**STOCK NUMBER**	**AVAILABILITY***
Desert Sand	101	All areas
Bark	102	All areas
Teakwood	103	1, 2, 3
Umber	104	All areas
Charcoal	105	1, 3, 4
Slate	106	All areas
Black	107	All areas
Mountain White	108	All areas
Gray-Green	109	4, 5, 6

* Numbers refer to regions serviced by our plants: 1 (Northeast), 2 (South), 3 (Midwest), 4 (Interior West), 5 (Northwest), 6 (Southwest).

14. What three kinds of information does the chart show?

    _____

    _____

    _____

15. What is the stock number of slate-colored shingles?

    _____

16. Where are charcoal-colored shingles available?

    _____

17. The owner of the house getting a new roof has decided on desert sand–colored shingles.
    Are they available in his area?

    _____

18. Where on the work order form should the stock number of the shingles be entered?

    _____

SERVICE: You have started work on a landscaping crew and have been given trees to plant. Below are instructions for planting them correctly.

To plant a balled-and-burlapped (B & B) tree:

Dig a hole approximately 10 in. deeper than the burlap ball is high and about 12 in. wider than the ball is wide. Fill the bottom 12 in. of the hole with fine, loosened soil to allow the roots to spread. Then place the B & B tree in the hole. **(See Diagram 1.)**

Mechanical cultivators at nurseries can toss up too much loose soil around the trunks of trees, depriving the roots of oxygen. To ensure this has not happened with a tree you are planting, loosen the top of the burlap bag and brush away the soil until the topmost roots are slightly exposed. Then roll the burlap down and away from the top of the root ball. **(See Diagram 2.)**

If the ball is true cloth burlap, leave it in place. The roots will grow through. But if it is plastic burlap, remove it at this point. Then fill in the hole with loosened soil.

Diagram 1.

Diagram 2.

19. The purpose of these instructions is to explain how to

    (1) wrap a tree in burlap
    (2) unwrap a tree in burlap
    (3) plant a tree
    (4) tend the roots of a tree

20. How deep should you dig a hole for a tree with a 20" burlapped root ball?

    _____

21. Number the steps in the order in which you should take them.

    ____ Loosen the burlap bag.
    ____ Place the tree in the hole.
    ____ Fill in the hole.
    ____ Roll the burlap down and away.
    ____ Dig the hole.
    ____ Fill the bottom 12" with loosened soil.
    ____ Brush away excess soil from the roots.
    ____ If plastic, remove the burlap.

22. Once you have followed the instructions, how many inches should there be between the surface of the ground and the top surface of the root ball?

    _____

23. What might happen if you do not brush excess soil from the top of the roots?

    (1) The tree will have to be replanted.
    (2) The roots will be deprived of oxygen.
    (3) The roots will not be able to spread.
    (4) The tree will die shortly.

24. Which of the following questions is answered by the instructions?

    (1) How wide should you dig the hole?
    (2) How can you tell if burlap is plastic?
    (3) How do you remove plastic burlap?
    (4) Should you water the tree?

Questions 25–26 are based on the following situation.

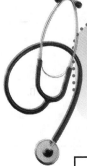

HEALTH CARE: You are working in a doctor's office and are told to fax some medical records to a hospital. But you have never used a fax machine before. So you find the manual and skim through it.

■ CONTENTS

25.   What are the main topics discussed in the manual?

_____

26.   On what page can you find out how to send a fax?

_____

Questions 27–28 are based on the following instructions for sending a fax.

■ SENDING A FAX AUTOMATICALLY

- To send a fax, first insert the paper or papers facedown in the document feeder.
- NOTE: Insert the top edge of the paper first into the feeder; otherwise, your fax will be received upside down.
- The message screen will change to read FAX: DIAL & START.
- Dial the fax number of the person you are sending the fax to. The number will appear on the message screen so that you can check to see if it is correct.
- Press START.

---

27. What should you do first?

_____

28. Suppose the fax does not go through the fax machine, and no signal appears on the message screen. Where can you look for help?

_____

Questions 29–30 are based on the following information from the "Problems and Care" section of the manual.

■ ERROR MESSAGE	■ CAUSE	■ WHAT TO DO
None—no signal	Receiver's fax is not working. Receiver's fax is out of paper.	Try sending again. Have other party check their machine
Change Cartridge	Cartridge is empty or low.	Replace the cartridge.
Check Paper	Paper jam or tray is empty.	Clear jam or add paper.
Check Front Cover	Front cover is open.	Close front cover.

29. What would you do first to solve the problem?

    (1) try sending the fax again
    (2) replace the cartridge
    (3) clear a jam or add paper
    (4) close the front cover

30. If the problem remains, what would you do?

    (1) wait and send the fax in a while
    (2) wait until the hospital calls you, and explain the situation
    (3) call the hospital to have them check their machine
    (4) tell the doctor you are having a fax problem

Skills Preview Answer Key

1. (2) to inform you how children at the center are treated
2. (3) The Kid's Corner program centers on children's needs.
3. (1) thinks and learns
4. (4) share
5. (2) note children's cubby, coat hanger, and cot assignments
6. (2) Juan
7. Lisa comes only in the mornings, and Jasmine comes only in the afternoons.
8. She probably no longer attends the center.
9. They were given to Erin.
10. (1) detail the tasks for putting a new roof on a house
11. J. Framer's
12. July 5
13. (4) the head of the work crew
14. The color, stock number, and availability of SealMate shingles.
15. 106
16. the Northeast, Midwest, and Interior West
17. Yes, desert sand-colored shingles are available in all areas.
18. under Materials
19. (3) plant a tree
20. 30" deep
21. 4, 3, 8, 6, 1, 2, 5, 7
22. 2"
23. (2) The roots will be deprived of oxygen.
24. (1) How wide should you dig the hole?
25. Setting Up, Know Your Machine, Sending Faxes, Receiving Faxes, Special Features, Problems and Care
26. page 27
27. insert the paper or papers facedown in the document feeder
28. in the table of contents under Problems and Care ("Troubleshooting") or in the Index
29. (1) try sending the fax again
30. (3) call the hospital to have them check their machine

Skills Preview Evaluation Chart

Circle the question numbers that you answered correctly. Then fill in the number of questions you got correct for each program lesson. Find the total number correct, and focus your work on the lessons you had trouble with.

Program Lesson	Question Number	Number Correct/Total
16: *Reading for a Purpose* Reading for Different Purposes, Using Different Approaches to Reading, Using Strategies to Understand What You Read	1, 2, 3, 4, 5, 6, 7, 8, 9	____/9
17: *Finding What You Need: Forms and Charts* Understanding Forms, Understanding Charts, Using Forms and Charts	10, 11, 12, 13, 14, 15, 16, 17, 18	____/9
18: *Following Directions* Reading Written Instructions, Interpreting Pictorial Instructions, Following Instructions	19, 20, 21, 22, 23, 24	____/6
19: *Reading Reports and Manuals* Becoming Familiar with Memos, Reports, and Workplace References; Finding the Information You Need; Using References Effectively	25, 26, 27, 28, 29, 30	____/6
	Total	____/30

Turn to page 12 to see what your score means.

If you got 27–30 correct: You have a strong foundation in the reading skills covered in this video series and workbook. Use the videos and workbook to further develop your skills.

If you got 24–26 correct: You have a basic knowledge of using reading skills in the workplace. Work carefully through this workbook to reinforce your skills.

If you got 21–23 correct: Through study and practice, you can improve your reading skills. As you improve your skills, you will be better prepared to meet the demands and challenges of any job.

If you got less than 21 correct: You need to learn more about using reading skills on the job. Use the information presented in the video programs and in this book to gain the knowledge and skills you need.

Remember to save your responses to this preview. After you have watched all the videos and completed the workbook lessons, you can take the Skills Review. When you compare your results on the review with your results here, you will see how much you have learned!

WATCH

Reading for a Purpose

The video program you are about to watch will
show you how basic reading skills are essential in
the workplace. This program will help you develop
an awareness of how reading effectively can mean
the difference between being an average worker and
an excellent worker.

As you watch, notice the different materials that people
read in the workplace. Watch for ways workers change
the way they read according to the kind of material they
are reading and what they need to learn from it. Also
notice strategies that people use for effective reading.

Think about the types of materials you read every day—
signs, product labels, menus, directories. Improving your
basic reading skills will help you not only at work but
also at home, at the store, and in your community.

Sneak Preview

This exercise previews some of the concepts from Program 16. After you answer the questions, use the Feedback on page 15 to help set your learning goals.

SERVICE: You have a new job waiting tables in a restaurant. In the server station, you are shown the following posted notice.

SIDE WORK FOR SERVERS ON A 3-SPLIT SHIFT	SIDE WORK FOR SERVERS ON A 4-SPLIT SHIFT
Section 1 Server: See side work for section 1 server on a 4-split shift.*	**Section 1 Server:** Clean coffee grinder and coffee machine and area under. Empty coffeepots and clean. Clean soda gun plastic catcher and area. Soak soda gun in pitcher of water. Clean iced tea container and put away. Put away lemons.
Section 2 Server: Wrap salad ingredients in plastic wrap and put in refrigerator. Cover dressings and put away. Clean salad bar area. Clean pie case inside and out. Wrap pies in plastic wrap and put in refrigerator. Clean soup machine, including counter and wall behind machine.*	**Section 2 Server:** Clean pie case inside and out. Wrap pies in plastic wrap and put in refrigerator. Clean soup machine, including counter and wall behind machine.
Section 3 Server: See side work for section 4 on a 4-split shift. Do the same except for refilling.*	**Section 3 Server:** Wrap salad ingredients in plastic wrap and put in refrigerator. Cover dressings and put away. Clean salad bar area.
* Every table in your section should be refilled with full napkin holder, salt, pepper, and sugar.	**Section 4 Server:** Refill everything on all tables—napkin holders, salt and pepper, sugar. Give all utensils and knives to Dale in kitchen to be cleaned. Clean and make sure ketchup bottles are full; marry ketchup. Empty and sort out breadbaskets and butters. Fill straws by soda and tea bags by coffee machine.

Answer these questions based on the server station notice.

1. The notice was written in order to

   (1) inform servers of the restaurant's sanitation policy
   (2) explain how to clean the pie case
   (3) direct servers what to do in addition to waiting on tables
   (4) explain how the restaurant is divided into sections

2. What should the server in section 4 do with all the utensils and knives?

  (1) clean them in the kitchen
  (2) give them to Dale
  (3) set them on the tables
  (4) put them away

3. What are the three main areas that the server in section 1 is responsible for?

  (1) the beverage areas: coffee, soda, and tea
  (2) the pie case, salad bar, and soup area
  (3) the coffee grinder, machine, and pots
  (4) napkin holders, salt and pepper, and sugar

4. In your own words, what do you think "marry ketchup" means?

  _____

Feedback

- If you got all of the answers right . . .
  you have a good foundation for reading effectively. When you watch the video, pay attention to the types of reading materials in the workplace and how workers change the way they read each type.

- If you missed question 1 . . .
  concentrate on identifying the purpose of a particular piece of reading material— why it was written and what you should be learning from it.

- If you missed question 2 . . .
  pay attention to how to find a particular piece of information you need.

- If you missed question 3 . . .
  focus on developing ways to better understand what you read, such as summing up ideas.

- If you missed question 4 . . .
  concentrate on ways to determine a word's meaning.

Vocabulary for *Reading for a Purpose*

attendance policy	a company's written plan and procedures for handling employee attendance
context clues	hints about the meaning of a word found in the surrounding words in the sentence or paragraph
e-mail	written communication sent by computer; short for *electronic mail*
icon	a small picture on a computer screen that stands for a program or command
main idea	the most important point a writer is making
manual	a small reference book, giving training on how to do something or information about a company and its policies. Sometimes called a handbook.
memo	a written communication in a business office; short for *memorandum*
menu	a list that appears on a computer screen from which the user can choose a program, command, or file
paycheck stub	a table that accompanies a paycheck and details income and deductions
resource	anything a person can use—a book, person, computer—to get needed information
safety policy	a company's written plan and guidelines for employee safety
scan	to move the eyes over a page of reading material, looking for key words or phrases, in order to locate specific information. To scan a chart or diagram, use column and row headings, labels, or keys to help locate information.
skim	to quickly read over any titles, headings, and pictures or charts that are included in a piece of reading material in order to get a sense of what it is about
strategies	methods a person can use to better understand what he or she reads
troubleshooter	a worker who locates problems and solves them

PBS LiteracyLink®

Now watch Program 16.

After you watch, work on:
- pages 17–32 in this workbook
- Internet activities at www.pbs.org/literacy

AFTER·you·WATCH

program **16**

Reading for a Purpose

On the following pages, you will learn more about the issues discussed in the video program and have an opportunity to develop and practice your skills.

Think About the Key Points from the Video Program

Understand that the purpose of workplace reading materials may be to:
- Inform you,
- Direct you, or
- Train you.

Depending on the kind of workplace material you are reading, you should:
- Adjust your reading speed.
- Skim titles, headings, captions, tables of contents, and so on.
- Scan to look for specific information.

To help you understand what you read, use **strategies** such as:
- Taking notes or highlighting.
- Restating what you have read.
- Using context clues.

WORKTIP

If you don't understand something you read on the job, you can:
- Reread it, using clues in the text to help you understand unfamiliar words.
- Look in a dictionary or other book that explains terms.
- Ask a co-worker or your supervisor.

Reading for Different Purposes

Understanding the Purpose of Reading Materials

Workers read a variety of materials on the job. **Memos, manuals,** and **schedules** are just a few of the many kinds of workplace materials you may need to read. An efficient reader—and worker—first **skims,** or quickly looks over, a piece of written material to determine its purpose. The reader asks, "What kind of reading material is this, and why was it written?" Skimming the material will help you determine whether the purpose of the information is to:

- Inform you about company matters.
- Direct you to do something.
- Train you regarding a job task, a work procedure, or a piece of equipment.

Skim the headings of the policy below, and then answer the questions.

TRI-TECH Manufacturing Company ▪ Attendance Policy

All employees must become familiar with our attendance policy. It is strictly enforced to ensure that stations on the assembly line are staffed at all times.

1. Procedures Must Be Followed for Tardiness

If you are unable to report to work at your scheduled time, you must call your supervisor as early as possible. Do not rely on others to pass the word. If you are not at your station at your scheduled time, you will be considered tardy. Being tardy three times will be treated as one absence.

2. Absences Must Be Approved

Employees who will be absent must provide a reason to their supervisor and have the absence approved. Approved absences include those for illness, family emergency, personal time off, and jury duty. Three unapproved absences in a 90-day period will result in a three-day suspension without pay.

1. What kind of workplace material do you think this is from?

    (1) order form

    (2) work schedule

    (3) employee handbook

    (4) training manual

2. The purpose of the writing is to

    (1) inform you about company policy

    (2) direct you to do something

    (3) train you in a specific task

    (4) explain a piece of equipment

Understanding Your Purpose for Reading

Once you understand why something was written, you will know your purpose for reading it. For example:

If you are reading—	your purpose usually is to—
• a general memo, policy manual, or employee handbook informing you of company matters	• find the main idea and key details
• a schedule informing you when you will work	• locate specific information
• a work order directing you to do something	• understand and follow instructions
• a manual or guide training you in a specific task or explaining a work procedure or piece of equipment	• learn and apply information

The **main idea** is the most important point a writer is making. Therefore, finding the main idea is often a reader's main purpose for reading. To find the main idea, first identify the topic. In a memo, the topic is often given right at the top of the page. The safety memo on page 119 shows you an example. In a longer piece of reading material, you can find the topic by looking at the title or main heading. Then read the first paragraph and any subheadings, or headings of sections, to find out what the writer is saying about the topic. That is the main idea.

Answer these questions about the employee handbook on page 18.

1. What would be your purpose for reading this part of the handbook?

   _____

2. What is the topic?

   _____

3. What is the main idea of section 1?

   _____

4. What is the main idea of section 2?

   _____

5. What is the main idea of this part of the handbook?

   _____

For more information on finding the main idea, turn to pages 120–122.

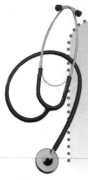

HEALTH CARE: Rashaan Masters is an SCA (Safety Control Assistant) at a local hospital. Rashaan's job is to help carry out the hospital **safety policy.** He often has to be a **troubleshooter**—a worker who locates problems and solves them. When Rashaan's boss, Amy Anderson, told him to run the daily check on the Health and Safety stations on each floor, Rashaan found the safety policy in the hospital manual. Then he located the section on Health and Safety stations.

Problem Solving

Read this page from the hospital manual and answer the questions.

Northern Bay Hospital Manual	Safety Policy	23

HEALTH AND SAFETY STATIONS

It is Northern Bay Hospital's policy to protect employees from exposure to harmful substances and the spread of disease, either airborne or through contact with skin or body fluids. To this end, the following Health and Safety stations are established and must be equipped at all times:

Eye Wash Stations
Eye wash stations are well marked and located in each hospital wing, as well as in the kitchen and laundry.

EPE Stations
In compliance with OSHA regulations and the Centers for Disease Control (CDC) guidelines, an Employee Protective Equipment (EPE) station is clearly marked in each hospital wing and contains the following EPE:

- 6 waterproof disposable gowns

- 1 box each non-allergenic latex gloves: small, medium, large

- 1 box High Efficiency Particulate Air (HEPA) masks
  (not to be used with known TB patients)

- 1 High Efficiency Particulate Air (HEPA) respirator
  (to be used with a known TB patient until being transferred)

- 1 pair goggles

- 1 CPR mask with one-way valve

1. What was Rashaan's purpose in reading this page?

   _____

2. What is the topic of the page?

   _____

3. List and explain two key details about the topic.

   _____

   _____

4. After Rashaan reads the manual, he must apply the information in it. How do you think he should proceed?

   _____

   _____

5. Upon inspection of the Health and Safety stations, Rashaan found the following potential problems:

   • The E Wing EPE station was low on medium-sized gloves.
   • A piece of kitchen equipment was partially blocking the sign and access to the eye wash station in the kitchen.

   What do you think Rashaan should do to solve these problems?

   _____

   _____

WRITE IT •

Help Rashaan write an **e-mail** message informing his supervisor, Amy Anderson, about the problems he located. After writing her name and the topic, write the main idea of his message. Then write the two key details. Write Rashaan's e-mail message here.

To:

Topic:

_____

_____

_____

_____

Using Different Approaches to Reading

Adjusting Your Speed

If you know your purpose for reading a piece of workplace material, you will know *how* you should read it. Some materials, such as training manuals or safety notices, should be read slowly and carefully. Other materials, such as general office memos, can be read quickly for the main idea and key points.

Decide how you would read each of the following workplace materials. Write *S* for slowly and carefully or *Q* for quickly.

_____ 1. a memo informing you about the company picnic

_____ 2. a work order instructing you to do a particular job

_____ 3. a manual explaining how to operate a piece of machinery

_____ 4. a section of the employee handbook on holidays and personal time

Skimming

It often helps to get a sense of an entire piece of reading material before you begin reading it. Skimming helps you do that. To skim, quickly read over any titles, headings, and pictures. In the last section, you skimmed short text materials. You can skim longer materials, such as a manual, by looking over the table of contents. You can also skim graphics such as charts and diagrams.

Below is a commonly used hospital chart. Skim the title and column headings to get a general idea of the document as a whole.

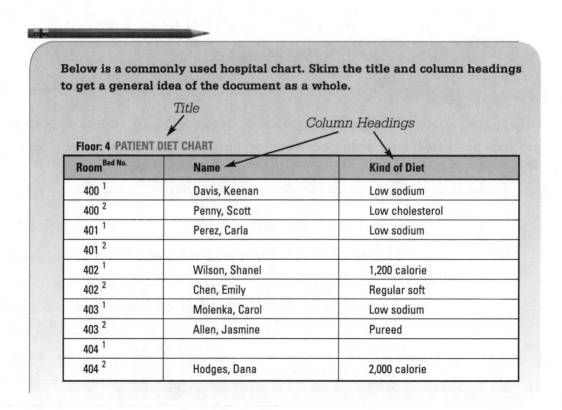

Title   *Column Headings*

Floor: 4 PATIENT DIET CHART

Room / Bed No.	Name	Kind of Diet
400 ¹	Davis, Keenan	Low sodium
400 ²	Penny, Scott	Low cholesterol
401 ¹	Perez, Carla	Low sodium
401 ²		
402 ¹	Wilson, Shanel	1,200 calorie
402 ²	Chen, Emily	Regular soft
403 ¹	Molenka, Carol	Low sodium
403 ²	Allen, Jasmine	Pureed
404 ¹		
404 ²	Hodges, Dana	2,000 calorie

1. What is the chart about? _____

2. What three types of information are included on the chart?

   _____   _____   _____

3. What do the small numbers ^{1} and ^{2} tell you?

   _____

Scanning

Sometimes you just want to find a piece of specific information in reading material. Scanning helps you do that quickly. To **scan,** move your eyes over the page, looking for key words or phrases. To scan a chart or diagram, use column and row headings, labels, or keys to help you locate information.

For example, here's how to scan to find the kind of special diet for the patient in room 402, bed 2, on the chart on page 22.

STEP 1: Locate the column listing the patient room numbers.
STEP 2: Scan down the column until you reach room 402^2. (Remember that the smaller 2 tells you that it's bed 2.)
STEP 3: Scan across row 402^2 until the row meets the column under the heading *Kind of Diet.*
STEP 4: Read the kind of diet needed: Regular soft foods.

Scan the diet chart on page 22 to answer the following questions.

1. What patient is on a low-cholesterol diet?

   _____

2. Who is in Bed 2, Room 403?

   _____

3. How many patients are on the low-sodium diet?

   _____

Scan the substance abuse policy on page 120 to locate the following pieces of information.

4. Is it all right to drink alcoholic beverages at Drew Construction?

   _____

5. When is drug testing done on employees?

   _____

SERVICE: May Sills is an insurance processing clerk at Optimum Insurance Company. When she received her first paycheck, she could not figure out how to read the **paycheck stub.** So she looked in her employee manual for help. May found a section called "Your Paycheck" that could help her.

Reading Strategies

Skim the sample paycheck stub and the key and codes at the bottom. Then scan to find the information that answers the questions that follow.

— HOW TO READ YOUR PAYCHECK STUB —

PAY STUB (1)

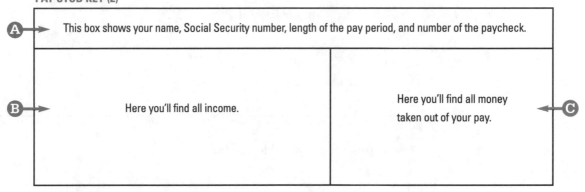

(A)

Employee Name	Soc. Sec. Number	Pay Period	Check No.
Joe Smith	000-00-0000	one week	00000

Payments

	Hours	Pay	YTD
Regular Earnings	35	350.00	700.00
OT Earnings	00	00.00	40.00
RPA		00.00	20.00
Total	**35**	**350.00**	**760.00**

Taxes and Deductions

Description	This Check	YTD
FIT	55.00	110.00
FICA	25.00	50.00
Medical/Dental	5.00	10.00
	85.00	**170.00**

(B) **(C)**

PAY STUB KEY (2)

(A) This box shows your name, Social Security number, length of the pay period, and number of the paycheck.

(B) Here you'll find all income.

(C) Here you'll find all money taken out of your pay.

PAY STUB CODES (3)

YTD	Year to Date	**RPA**	Retroactive Pay Adjustment	**EXP**	Expenses
OT	Overtime Pay	**FIT**	Federal Income Tax	**FICA**	Social Security Tax

1. Into what three sections is this diagram divided?

_____

2. According to the sample paycheck stub, what is listed in the section labeled B?

_____

3. According to the "Pay Stub Codes" section, what does FIT stand for?

_____

Now compare May's pay stub with the sample on page 24. Skim and scan the diagram to answer the questions.

Employee Name	Soc. Sec. Number	Pay Period	Check No.		
May Sills	000-00-8768	6/1–6/15	20167		
Payments				**Taxes and Deductions**	
	Hours	Pay	YTD	Description	This Check	YTD
Regular Earnings	75	750.00	9,475.00	FIT	132.00	1,452.00
OT Earnings	10	150.00	2,500.00	FICA	66.00	207.00
RPA		10.00	450.00	Medical/ Dental	12.05	120.59
Total	85	910.00	12,425.00		210.05	1,779.59

4. How much did May make in regular earnings this pay period?

_____

5. How much were her overtime earnings this pay period?

_____

6. What taxes and deductions were taken out of May's pay this pay period? Explain what the letters stand for.

_____

7. What does the amount $450 represent on the stub?

_____

TECH TIP

You use skimming and scanning often when you use a computer. For example, when you turn on a computer, a **menu** of programs, files, or commands appears on the screen. Sometimes the menu lists words only; sometimes the menu consists of small **icons,** or pictures, that stand for programs, files, or commands. Refer to page 123 for more information on a computer menu. Practice skimming and scanning the one shown. If you like, use a computer at a library to practice skimming and scanning menus of word-processing programs and on-line services.

Using Strategies to Understand What You Read

Developing Comprehension Strategies

To be an effective worker, you must be an active reader. Reading actively involves using strategies such as these before and as you read:

- Knowing your purpose for reading
- Skimming to preview reading material
- Taking notes or highlighting
- Restating the key points to yourself
- Checking your understanding as you read and rereading if necessary
- Thinking of an example of a key point
- Picturing, or visualizing, what you read

For example, here is a paragraph from a bank teller's training manual with strategies you can use as you read.

THE HAND-TO-COUNTER METHOD OF COUNTING OUT MONEY ◄ ── **1**

Do not look the customer in the eye when using the hand-to-counter method. Instead, focus on your hands. Start by placing the bills, highest on top, in the hand opposite the one you write with. Then one by one, using your other hand, take the bills off the top of the pile and place them in a pile on the countertop in front of you. You may count out loud or to yourself as you place the bills down. Look at the entire bill as it passes from one hand to the other and to the counter. In this way, you can also check for any torn or worn bills or counterfeits. ◄ ── **3**

} ── **2**

---

1 *Strategy:* Set a purpose: "I am going to learn one way to count money."

2 *Strategy:* Picture how the pile of money should be held in your hand. Picture yourself taking each bill off and placing it down.

3 *Strategy:* Ask yourself, "What did I just read?" Try to restate the purpose in your own words. If you can't, go back and reread.

Use the strategies to answer these questions.

1. What would be your purpose in reading this passage?

   _____

2. Picture yourself using this method. If you are a right-handed person, which of your hands is holding the pile of money?

   _____

3. Tell someone how to use the hand-to-counter method of counting money. Demonstrate for them.

Developing Vocabulary Strategies

When you come across an unfamiliar word in your workplace reading, there are several ways to find out the word's meaning:

- Ask a co-worker or your supervisor
- Use context clues
- Look up the word in a **resource,** such as the glossary of a manual or a dictionary.

Context clues are found in the surrounding words in the sentence or paragraph. A clue can be a definition, an explanation, or just the overall sense of the sentence. Page 124 gives further information on context clues.

Here are some directions from a sewing manual. Look for the meaning of each bold (dark) word in the words that surround it. Underline the words that give a clue to the bold word's meaning.

1. If you look at a piece of fabric, you will notice that the fibers all go in one direction. Make sure you check this **grain** line when cutting out pieces from fabric.

2. Make sure to match **selvage** edges with other finished edges because you don't want to mix finished edges with unfinished edges that will fray.

3. Press the hip **dart** before sewing. This stitched fold of fabric will give shape and style to a front piece or pants.

4. Make sure the **tolerance** does not exceed $\pm\frac{1}{8}"$. If you have no seam allowance between the sewing line and the cutting line, you may cut into the fabric piece.

Now use a dictionary to check your ideas about the meanings of the bold words above. Use your knowledge of alphabetical order and the guide words at the top of each spread of pages in the dictionary to locate each word. Then choose the definition that best fits the context of the sentence above. Does it match your idea of the word's meaning?

You may wish to refer to page 125 for information on how to use the dictionary.

MANUFACTURING: Rich Contrera works in the warehouse of an appliance manufacturer. The instructions below are posted in the warehouse. Rich must follow them when using a forklift to move appliances to the shipping dock.

Reading Strategies

Use reading and vocabulary strategies as you read the following safety notice.

FORKLIFT SAFETY

HOW TO PICK UP A LOAD
Follow these steps:
1. Find out how much weight your forklift can handle before you pick up the load. Never exceed the suggested weight.
2. Make sure the bands around the load are secure.
3. Set the forks as wide as possible for the particular load.
4. Square up to the load, and approach it slowly.
5. Level the forks and raise them to the bottom of the load.
6. Drive forward slowly until the load lies against the backrest of the forklift.
7. Raise the load 6 to 8 inches.
8. Tilt the mast, or support pole, to stabilize the load, ensuring that it will not fall.
9. Back up slowly and carefully.

HOW TO DRIVE WITH A LOAD
Always remember that you are carrying a load where people may be walking and where appliances and other valuable goods are stored. Drive with your vision cleared 360 degrees. Be sure that there are no obstacles on the floor or overhead that can block your path or get in your way. Never travel with a raised load. Drive at a safe speed at all times. It is a good practice to keep three forklift lengths behind any vehicle. Use your horn at intersections or where there may be workers who are unaware that that the forklift is coming through.

HOW TO SET DOWN A LOAD
Follow these steps:
1. Square up to the stack, pallet, or other unloading spot, and approach it slowly.
2. Raise the load so that it clears the unloading spot, and drive slowly forward.
3. Position the load over the unloading spot.
4. Tilt the mast forward until it is vertical.
5. Lower the load smoothly until it comes to rest.
6. Free the forks, and back up slowly and carefully.

1. What purpose would Rich set for reading these instructions?

   _____

2. Skimming the instructions would tell Rich that he was going to read about what three main topics?

   _____

3. **a.** In your own words, restate what this instruction means: "Always drive with your vision cleared 360 degrees."

   _____

   b. Restate what this instruction means: "Square up to the load."

   _____

4. Which of these pictures shows the correct way to drive with a load?

   (1)    **(2)**

5. Try to use context clues to answer the following questions.

   a. What does the word *mast* mean as it is used in these instructions?

   _____

   b. What does the word *stabilize* mean as it is used in these instructions?

   _____

   c. What does the word *obstacle* mean as it is used in these instructions?

   _____

WRITE IT ·

Keep your own personal dictionary of special vocabulary you need on the job. Use the chart on page 126. In the first column, list words you come across in workplace reading materials. In the second column, write the definition of each word and/or a sentence showing how it is used.

Review

You have learned some basic skills for reading effectively on the job: identifying different purposes for reading, using different approaches to reading, and using strategies while you are reading. These skills are outlined on page 127, "The Reading Process." This Program Review will give you a chance to see how well you can apply these basic skills.

The following page is from a bulletin board notice in an automotive service center. Skim it to get an overall idea of what it is about. Then read it and answer the questions that follow.

AUTOMOTIVE TRAINING FOR CLARK'S TECHNICIANS

To keep up with the demand for automobile service technicians, Clark's Automotive Center has arranged for our employees to take courses leading to a certificate in automotive service technology. Here is a course listing.

JOB	DESCRIPTION	QUALIFICATIONS	TRAINING COURSES
MECHANIC	Handles routine maintenance tasks	High school diploma or GED; interest in cars	*Basic Auto Mechanics I and **II Tues. & Thurs. 3–5
TECHNICIAN	Specialized tasks	Two years of auto mechanic experience and–	See specific course areas below:
• Tune-ups	Use diagnostic equipment and other computerized devices to locate malfunctions	Electronic aptitude and troubleshooting skills	*Tune-up Basics **Advanced Tune-up Mon. & Wed. 1–3
• Electrical systems	Service and repair electrical and computer circuitry in newer-model cars	Some postsecondary training; basic mechanical aptitude	*Electrical Circuitry **Computer Circuitry Tues. & Thurs. 1–3
• Brake repair	Work on drum and disk braking systems, parking brakes and their hydraulic systems	Course in front-end specialty	**Basic Brake Repair Mon. & Wed. 3–5

* Courses begin October 1 and run through December 31.
** Courses begin January 15 and run through April 15.

QUALIFICATIONS FOR THE COURSE PROGRAM

To qualify for these company prepaid courses, you must have worked for Clark's for at least six months and demonstrated an aptitude for automobile technology and repair. You must have a high school diploma or show evidence that you are enrolled in a GED (General Educational Development) program. Some formal training in automotive work is preferred.

HOW TO REGISTER FOR THE PROGRAM

If you would like to apply for one of these courses, get an application from Human Resources. Applications must be filled out and submitted by August 15. Make sure that you have listed all work experience and work-related training carefully. Notification of approval will be given by August 30.

1. The purpose of the bulletin board notice is to

    (1) inform you about a company training policy
    (2) direct you to repair a car
    (3) train you to perform a specific automotive job task
    (4) explain an automotive work procedure

2. Skimming tells you that the entire notice will give you information about which three topics?

    _____

    _____

    _____

3. Skimming tells you that the course chart gives you information on which four topics?

    _____

    _____

4. Would you read the notice fairly quickly, or slowly and carefully? Why?

    _____

5. Which of the following statements is the main idea of the notice?

    (1) Clark's must keep up with the demand for automotive service technicians.
    (2) Clark's has arranged for employees to take courses leading to a certificate in automotive service technology.
    (3) You must have a high school diploma or GED or show evidence that you are enrolled in a GED program.
    (4) Work experience and work-related training must be listed carefully.

6. What is the difference between a mechanic and a technician?

_____

_____

_____

7. Write *True* if the statement is true; *False* if it is false.

_____ a. An electrical system technician needs no computer training.

_____ b. Brake repairers need to have had a course in front-end work.

_____ c. There are two levels of Basic Auto Mechanics courses.

_____ d. Everyone who takes a course will earn a certificate in automotive service technology.

_____ e. You must be enrolled in a GED program to take an automotive course.

_____ f. Clark's is paying for the courses.

8. Scan the notice to find the following pieces of information. Check each statement that is true.

____ a. Basic Auto Mechanics I runs from October 1 to December 31.

____ b. To qualify to be a technician, you must have been a mechanic for three years.

____ c. Computer Circuitry is given Tuesdays and Thursdays from 1 to 3.

____ d. An application can be obtained from your supervisor.

____ e. Applications must be submitted by August 30.

9. Ron Urbanski has worked as a mechanic at Clark's for three years. The manager often calls Ron in to diagnose tough problems.

a. For which job might Ron qualify?

_____

b. What courses should he take?

_____

10. Noah Martin has a high school diploma. He often fixes his own car. He helped out at Clark's on weekends and after school during his last two years of school.

a. For which job might Noah qualify?

_____

b. What courses should Noah take?

_____

BEFORE YOU WATCH

program **17**

WATCH

Finding What You Need: Forms and Charts

The video program you are about to watch will show you a variety of forms and charts that are commonly used in the workplace. This program will help you develop an awareness of the importance and usefulness of forms and charts found on the job.

As you watch, notice the kind of information that different forms ask for and the way information is organized on charts. You will see how important it is to read and fill out forms and charts carefully so that accurate information is transmitted.

Forms and charts are convenient tools for use at home, at school, and in the workplace. As you watch the video, think about how often you fill out or read forms and charts in your daily life.

Sneak Preview

This exercise previews some of the concepts from Program 17. After you answer the questions, use the Feedback on page 35 to help set learning goals.

MANUFACTURING: You work in the human resources department of a large bakery that supplies stores in your region. It is your responsibility to screen employment applications and file them according to the positions that are available. Here is one application that comes across your desk.

EMPLOYMENT APPLICATION			
Arias LAST NAME	*Juan* FIRST NAME	*S* MIDDLE INITIAL	*(777) 555-1313* TELEPHONE NO.
666 Filmore Street ADDRESS STREET		*Newton, KY* TOWN/CITY	*09456* ZIP CODE
3/5/78 BIRTH DATE		*000-11-0010* S.S. NO.	

AVAILABILITY AND TYPE OF EMPLOYMENT

Date available ___*Immediately*___

	M	T	W	Th	F	S
From	2	6	2	9	9	9
To	9	9	9	9	9	9

❏ Seasonal   ✓ Regular FT   ❏ Temporary PT

POSITION APPLYING FOR:

❏ Sales   ✓ Local Delivery   ❏ Production Line
❏ Interstate Delivery   ❏ Maintenance   ❏ Shipping and Handling

Answer the following only if the position for which you are applying requires driving.
Are you licensed to drive?   ✓ Yes   ❏ No
Is your license valid in Kentucky?   ✓ Yes   ❏ No
Has your license ever been revoked?   ❏ Yes   ✓ No   If, yes, explain. _____

Special skills and experience related to the job you are applying for:
Florist delivery person using company van for 6 months

Answer these questions based on the employment application.

1. What is the main purpose of this form?

_____

2. What hours is Juan Arias available to work on Wednesdays?

_____

3. Suppose you may want to hire Juan Arias for the position of Local Delivery Driver. Check the four pieces of information you think are most important to consider.

_____ Name   _____ Availability

_____ Telephone number   _____ Position applying for

_____ Address   _____ Driving information

_____ Birth date   _____ Special skills and experience

_____ Social Security number

4. What might happen if Juan Arias mistakenly checked Interstate Delivery instead of Local Delivery?

_____

Feedback

- If you got all of the answers right . . .   you have a good foundation for working with forms and charts. When you watch the video, note the variety of forms and charts used on the job and note any tips or hints to improve your reading.

- If you missed question 1 . . .   focus on understanding the purpose of forms that you use.

- If you missed question 2 . . .   study how to read charts and find specific information on them.

- If you missed question 3 . . .   concentrate on determining which information on a particular form is essential.

- If you missed question 4 . . .   pay attention to what can happen if a form or chart is filled incorrectly.

....

Vocabulary for *Finding What You Need: Forms and Charts*

database	a collection of information that can be organized in different ways
field	an area in a computerized form, sometimes appearing as a colored box, which requires a specific piece of information
inventory	a list of the goods that a store or business currently has in stock
keyboard	the part of a computer with letters, numbers, and function keys for inputting information
monitor	the part of a computer with a screen that displays stored information
purchase order	a form used to list one or more items to buy
work schedules	charts showing employees' assigned work hours

PBS LiteracyLink®

Now watch Program 17.

After you watch, work on:
- pages 37–52 in this workbook
- Internet activities at www.pbs.org/literacy

AFTER you WATCH

program **17**

Finding What You Need: Forms and Charts

On the following pages, you will learn more about the issues discussed in the video program and have an opportunity to develop your skills.

Think About the Key Points from the Video

When you read a form:
- Know what the form is used for.
- Skim first, then read carefully.
- Determine which pieces of information are most essential.

When you read a chart:
- Know what the chart is used for.
- Read the headings at the tops of columns and beginnings of rows.
- If necessary, use a highlighter or ruler to find information.

When you fill in a form or chart:
- Know what information needs to be included.
- Fill in the information accurately.
- Double-check your work.

Understanding Forms

Reviewing Common Forms

As the video showed, forms are part of your everyday life. On the day you were born, a form was filled out for you. It was your birth certificate. Since then, you have probably filled out forms yourself for a variety of personal needs. You may have filled out forms to obtain a driver's license, to apply for a job or a credit card, or to order something from a catalog. Each form has a different purpose.

Study the form below and answer the questions that follow.

CHANGE OF ADDRESS

Old Information

Name _____

Street Address _____

City, State, ZIP Code _____

New Information

Name _____

Street Address _____

City, State, ZIP Code _____

Date to Stop Delivering Mail to Old Address _____/_____/_____

1. You would fill out this form if you were planning to

   (1) look for a job
   (2) get a marriage license
   (3) move to a new house or apartment
   (4) buy a home

2. Who would you give this form to?

   _____

Identifying Workplace Forms

You will probably see and use a variety of forms on the job. In fact, for some jobs, you might need to read the same kind of form that you fill out as a customer. For example, a customer service representative for a catalog company reads the order forms sent in by customers. For many jobs, you need to read forms completed by workers in your department or other departments.

Match the type of form with the department that would be most likely to use the form.

Type of Form

_____ 1. Order form

_____ 2. Billing form

_____ 3. Shipping form

_____ 4. Job application

_____ 5. Quality control form

Workplace Department

a. Manufacturing or production

b. Mailroom

c. Customer service

d. Human resources

e. Accounting

Reading a Form

Like everyday forms, each workplace form has its own purpose. To achieve that purpose, it asks for specific pieces of information. When reading a form for the first time, skim it first to understand its purpose. Then read each line carefully so that you know what information is required.

Suppose you are the postal worker who accepts the Change of Address form on page 38. What essential information does the form give you? Check all that apply.

_____ 1. Phone number

_____ 2. Old address

_____ 3. Date of birth

_____ 4. New address

_____ 5. Date that the customer plans to move

_____ 6. Social Security number

SERVICE: Louise Jones works at a hotel. Her job includes admitting guests and assisting them by making reservations, taking messages, and so on. Every two weeks she must submit a time request form to her supervisor. It is important that she fill out the form accurately so that few changes are needed after the schedule has been made.

Reading Strategies

Note the abbreviations that are used on the time request form. Notice too that a day off on a hotel schedule can be any day of the week. A typical workday is usually seven or eight hours.

Read the form below and answer the questions.

T I M E   R E Q U E S T   F O R M

Name ___Louise Jones___ Date ___August 7___

Department ___Concierge___ Supervisor ___C. Gregopolis___

Please enter the date after each day and write the number of work hours below.
Forms must be submitted to your supervisor by the Monday before the new schedule period.

DO: Day off **V:** Vacation Day **H:** Holiday **P:** Personal Day

| Mon 8/13 | Tues 8/14 | Wed 8/15 | Thur 8/16 | Fri 8/17 | Sat 8/18 | Sun 8/19 | |
| Hrs 8 | 8 | 8 | 8 | 8 | DO | DO | Total 40 |

| Mon 8/20 | Tues 8/21 | Wed 8/22 | Thur 8/23 | Fri 8/24 | Sat 8/25 | Sun 8/26 | |
| Hrs P | 8 | 8 | DO | DO | 8 | 8 | Total 32 |

Associate's Signature ___Louise Jones___

---

1. What is the purpose of this form?

    _____

2. Which departments of the hotel might need to use the information on this form? Check all that apply.

    ____ **a.** Concierge   ____ **d.** Payroll

    ____ **b.** Maintenance   ____ **e.** Maid service

    ____ **c.** Scheduling   ____ **f.** Room service

3. Which day does Louise want to take off as a personal day?

_____

4. The first week Louise requested the weekend off. Which days does she want off the second week?

_____

5. How many hours does Louise schedule for each week?

_____

6. Did Louise's supervisor approve her time request? How do you know?

_____

7. Suppose you usually work 40 hours a week in the concierge department. For the week beginning Monday, September 10, you want Thursday and Friday off. The second week you need Friday off for a personal day and want Saturday and Sunday off. Fill out the form below to reflect your requested hours.

DO: Day off   **V:** Vacation Day   **H:** Holiday   **P:** Personal Day

Mon _____ Tues _____ Wed _____ Thur _____ Fri _____ Sat _____ Sun _____
Hrs _____   _____   _____   _____   _____   _____   _____ Total _____

Mon _____ Tues _____ Wed _____ Thur _____ Fri _____ Sat _____ Sun _____
Hrs _____   _____   _____   _____   _____   _____   _____ Total _____

Associate's Signature _____

TECH TIP •

Today, many forms in the workplace are kept on computer. While paper forms are filled in with a pen or pencil, information on a computerized form is typed in, or input, with the computer **keyboard** and read on the **monitor.** Each piece of information is entered into a specific **field,** sometimes appearing as a colored box. You can see an example of a form as it would appear on a computer on page 128. As a customer, you can practice working with computerized forms to order merchandise or locate items in certain stores, to request books from the library, or to request information through an Internet service.

Understanding Charts

Reviewing Common Charts

As you remember from the video, using charts is a common and convenient way to find information that you need to know. TV listings and tax tables are just a few of the charts you may use. A schedule is a kind of chart too. Each chart organizes a particular kind of information and is used for a particular purpose.

Look at the bus schedule below. Skim the title and the headings. Then answer the questions that follow.

SUMMER BUS SCHEDULE
June–August • Bus No. 268

TO LODI (EAST)				FROM LODI (WEST)			
Tilden	Rugby	Dumott	Lodi	Lodi	Dumott	Rugby	Tilden
A.M.	A.M.	A.M.	A.M.	A.M.	A.M.	A.M.	A.M.
6:10	6:30	6:45	7:30	6:20	7:05	7:20	7:40
7:10	7:30	7:45	8:30	7:20	8:05	8:20	8:40
10:20	10:40	10:55	11:40	10:20	11:05	11:20	11:40
P.M.	P.M.	P.M.	P.M.	P.M.	P.M.	P.M.	P.M.
4:15	4:35	4:50	5:40	4:00	4:45	5:00	5:20
4:45	5:05	5:20	6:05	4:30	5:15	5:30	5:50

Write *True* if the statement is true; *False* if it is false.

_____ 1. You could use this schedule the year round.

_____ 2. This schedule includes trips between Tilden and Ridgefield.

_____ 3. This schedule shows morning and afternoon trips between Tilden and Lodi.

_____ 4. This is a round-trip schedule between Tilden and Lodi.

Recognizing Workplace Charts

Many companies have employee **work schedules** in the form of charts. You can see an example of one on page 129. Workplace charts also include production schedules, maintenance charts, and price lists. Can you think of any other workplace charts you have come across?

Skim the following work schedule for assistant managers at a fast-food restaurant, and then answer the questions.

WORK SCHEDULE Week of 8/13 – 8/19	ASST.MGR.	MON 8/13	TUES 8/14	WED 8/15	THUR 8/16	FRI 8/17	SAT 8/18	SUN 8/19
	Karen	6:30 AM–3:30 PM	6:30 AM–3:30 PM	3:30 PM–12 AM	3:30 PM–12 AM	OFF	OFF	6:30 AM –3:30 PM
	Chris	3:30 PM–12 AM	3:30 PM–12 AM	OFF	OFF	6:30 AM–3:30 PM	6:30 AM–3:30 PM	3:30 PM –12 AM
	Alonzo	OFF	OFF	6:30 AM–3:30 PM	6:30 AM–3:30 PM	3:30 PM–12 AM	3:30 PM–12 AM	OFF

1. What is the purpose of this chart?

_____

2. Why is this chart necessary?

_____

Reading a Chart

To understand a chart, follow these steps:

1. Read the title. This will tell you what the information on the chart is used for.

2. Skim the headings at the top of the columns and along the side of the rows. These will tell you how the information is organized.

Now you can look up specific information. For example, look at the work schedule above. To find who is working Tuesday from 3:30 P.M. to midnight, follow these steps:

3. Scan down the column under Tuesday until you find 3:30 P.M.–12 A.M.

4. Follow that row left back to the employee's name—Chris.

Some people find that using their finger, a ruler, or a highlighter helps them track the information across a row.

Refer to the chart above to answer the questions.

1. What hours does Karen work on Monday? _____

2. Who is the nighttime assistant manager on Friday? _____

3. Karen calls in sick at noon on Thursday, August 16. If you are the manager of the restaurant, whom would you call in to take her place and why?

_____

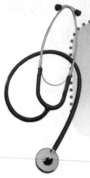

HEALTH CARE: Megan Scully works in the kitchen at a local hospital. Megan's job is to prepare the patients' food trays. She must follow dietary charts to make sure that patients' meals are prepared according to their doctors' specifications.

Reading Strategies

Here is part of one of the daily dietary charts that Megan reads.

Skim the dietary chart below. Then scan to answer the questions that follow.

Daily Dietary Chart

DAY: Tuesday   **MEAL:** Breakfast

Meal Plan	Milk	Fruits & Vegetables	Grains & Breads	Protein
High-Fiber Diet	2% 1 cup	4–6 oz. o.j.	1 c. cold cereal 1 bran muffin 1 sl. dt. wh. bread	1 scrambled egg
Low Sodium Diet	2% 1 cup	4–6 oz. o.j.	1 c. cold cereal 1 bran muffin 1 sl. dt. wh. bread	1 scrambled egg
1200-Calorie Diet	Skim 1 cup	4 oz. o.j. nonsweet	$\frac{3}{4}$ c. cold cereal 1 diet bran muffin 1 sl. dt. wh. bread	1 hard-boiled egg
2000-Calorie Diet	2% 1 cup	8 oz. o.j. nonsweet	$1\frac{1}{2}$ c. cold cereal 1 bran muffin 1 sl. dt. wh. bread	1 scrambled egg
Low-Cholesterol Diet (275–325mg)	Skim 1 cup	8 oz. o.j.	1 c. cornflakes 1 bran muffin 1 sl. dt. wh. bread	No-yolk eggs

1. For what day and meal should Megan use this chart?

   _____

2. What is the source of protein on all diets?

   _____

3. What is the source of fruit on the diets?

   _____

4. a. What does "1 sl. dt. wh. bread" refer to under Grains and Breads?

   _____

   b. What could Megan do if she did not know what the abbreviations meant?

   _____

5. Mrs. Regina Hadley in Room 208 is on a low-sodium diet. What foods should Megan put on her tray?

   _____

6. Which diet requires skim milk and no-yolk eggs? Why do you think this is so?

   _____

7. Compare the 1,200-calorie and the 2,000-calorie meal plans. Explain the reason for the different amounts and types of food.

   _____

8. Write *True* if a statement is true; *False* if it is false.

   _____ a. There is no difference between a high-fiber and a low-sodium breakfast.
   _____ b. Diet wheat bread is served with all the breakfasts listed.
   _____ c. Skim milk is served with a 2,000-calorie diet.
   _____ d. Orange juice is a high-cholesterol food.

MATH MATTERS ●

Like Megan's dietary aide job, many jobs require measuring amounts. Look at the chart below. It lists some measurements Megan uses in her job and their abbreviations. Use a copy of the chart on page 126 to make your own list of measurements you work with on the job or at home. You might also want to include measurement equivalents, such as 1 cup equals 8 ounces. Keep your chart as a handy reference.

Measure	Abbreviation
cup	c
ounce	oz
gram	g
milligram	mg

Using Forms and Charts

Forms and charts are helpful in the workplace, but only if they are completed and interpreted correctly.

Completing Forms and Charts

Below is a telephone conversation between Dwight Small, an apartment tenant, and Miranda Lewis, the manager of his apartment building:

Lewis: Lakeview Apartments. How may I help you?

Small: This is Dwight Small in Apartment 4F. I'm having a problem with my air conditioner. It doesn't work, and it's leaking water.

Lewis: I'm sorry, Mr. Small—

Small: Can you have it fixed right away? With this hot weather, I'm worried about our baby.

Lewis: We'll have it fixed within 24 hours. I wish I could make it sooner, but with this heat wave, we've been flooded with calls.

When the manager takes a call from a tenant with a problem, she uses a Tenant Complaint Form, shown on the next page, to record the information.

Complete the *top* portion of the form as Miranda would with information from the conversation.

Interpreting Information

Dave Gray is head of maintenance at Lakeview Apartments. He takes the Tenant Complaint Form from his In box in the manager's office. He reads the problem description and the priority. Then he assigns the job to Bill Smoltz, a custodial engineer, and hands Bill the form.

Answer these questions about the form.

1. By what time should Bill repair the air conditioner?

   _____

2. Bill arrives at the apartment at 10:30 A.M. on July 6. He replaces a bad valve on the air conditioner, then checks it out to make sure it's working. When he finishes, the time is 11 A.M. Complete the bottom of the form as Bill should complete it.

3. Who also needs to write on the form once Bill has solved the problem?

   _____

TENANT COMPLAINT FORM

Problem Log# __75__

Call taken by __Miranda Lewis__   Date __7-5__   Time __6:30 p.m.__

Tenant's Name _____   Apt._____

Problem Description _____

- [ ] Priority 1 (handle in 1 hour)   [ ] Priority 3 (handle in 3 days)
- [X] Priority 2 (handle in 24 hours)   [ ] Priority 4 (handle in 14 days)

Referred to   [ ] Landscaping   [X] Custodial   [ ] Electrical   [ ] Plumbing

Name of engineer servicing problem __BILL SMOLTZ__

Action Taken _____

Date/Time Resolved _____   Hours Spent _____

Upon Resolution: Tenant's Initials _____   Supervisor's Initials _____

Understanding the Importance of Accuracy

Information on a form or chart cannot be interpreted correctly unless it is accurately recorded in the first place. Filling out a form or chart incorrectly can result in the loss of service to a customer, workers' time, and your company's money. If you are filling out a paper form or chart, use a dark pencil or a pen, and be sure that each letter can be read. Whether filling out a paper or a computerized form or chart, always double-check your work.

Answer the following questions about the Tenant Complaint Form above.

1. What might happen if Miranda Lewis writes the wrong apartment number on the form?

   _____

2. What might happen if Bill Smoltz forgets to have the tenant initial the form?

   _____

SALE
SALE

RETAIL: Tyler Bonds is a sales associate in a bookstore. Part of his job is to help customers find books and to answer their questions. He also has to use the cash register to total customers' purchases and make change. When the **inventory** of books runs low, Tyler must fill out a **purchase order** and send it to the publisher. A purchase order is a request to buy listed supplies or equipment.

Problem Solving

Tyler's boss tells him to complete a purchase order for two titles.

Use the purchase order below to answer the questions and do the activity.

PURCHASE ORDER   No. 3492

To Williams Publishing Company

Address 1234 Randolph Street, Chicago, Illinois 60601

Phone 1-312-555-1999

Ship To Book Nook

Address 339 Best Street, Iowa City, Iowa 33539

Phone 1-319-555-7777

Date Required 9/15   **How Ship** UPS   **Terms** 30 Days

Title	Author	ISBN	Quantity	Unit Price	Cost
Goldfish	Fiene	5967-9367-9	5	5.95	
Fly Fishing	Conover	6367-9343-1	3	12.95	

Send 3 copies of your invoice. Thank you, _____, **Purchasing Agent**

---

1. The purchase order number is _____

2. The terms of payment are that Book Nook will pay within _____ days.

3. What missing information does Tyler need to find and fill in to complete this purchase order form?

   _____

4. If the publishing company representative has a question about this order, what phone number should he or she call?

   _____

5. From the form, you can infer that the ISBN is

   (1) the date that the book was published   (3) the number of pages

   (2) an identification number for each book   (4) the author's Social Security number

TECH TIP ··

To find information needed to complete the purchase order, Tyler uses the store's computerized **database.** A database is a collection of information that can be easily organized in different ways, depending on the purpose.

Look at the partial database display below. Each column is a field in which information can be entered.

Fields

```
            BOOK NOOK INVENTORY CONTROL
TITLE         AUTHOR        PUBLISHER       PRICE      IN STOCK
FISHING       BOONE         VENTURE         15.95        1
FLY FISHING   FIENE         WILLIAMS         5.95        1
FLYING        CONOVER       WILLIAMS        12.95        0
GOLF          HORAN         YELLEN           7.95        2
```

1. The database is currently organized alphabetically by which field? _____

2. Tyler's manager tells him to check the Inventory Control database to find out which other books are closest to running out. Tyler should reorganize the database and look at it by using which field?

   _____

Review

You have just read and filled out different types of forms. You have seen how to read and complete charts. You learned the importance of using forms and charts carefully so that accurate information is communicated. This Program Review will give you a chance to see how well you can apply this knowledge and these skills.

Suppose you work in a real estate office. Your boss needs papers for the closing of a sale on a house shipped to an associate in a nearby town for the next morning. She gives you a folder with about 50 pages in it, including some legal-sized, $8\frac{1}{2}$ in. $\times$ 14 in. documents. She hands you the partially completed form below and tells you any packaging you may need is in the office mailroom.

Skim the form below, and then answer the questions.

SHIPPING LABEL	
FROM:	**PACKAGE SERVICE**
Date Internal Reference No. *C21*	Next Day A.M. ☐ Next Day P.M. ☐ Two-Day ☐
Name	**FREIGHT SERVICE**
Company	Next Day ☐ Two-Day ☐ Three-Day ☐
Address	**PACKAGING**
City State ZIP Code	Letter ☐ Box ☐ Pack ☐ Tube ☐
TO:	**PAYMENT** Bill to:
Name	Sender ☑ Recipient ☐ Third Party ☐
Company	Account No.
Address	*549-02-371*
City State ZIP Code	Credit Card No.
For Saturday Delivery, check here ☐	
Signature	Total Packages
	Total Weight

1. What is the purpose of this form?

   _____

2. In general, what information goes in the upper left section of the form?

   (1) about the sender
   (2) about the recipient
   (3) about the contents
   (4) about the service required

3. In general, what information goes in the bottom left section of the form?

   (1) about the sender
   (2) about the recipient
   (3) about the contents
   (4) about the service required

4. What do you think Internal Reference Number might refer to?

   (1) the date the package is to be received
   (2) the weight of the package
   (3) an accounting number, to help identify the charge when it is received
   (4) a tracking number, in case the package gets lost

5. If today is Wednesday, should you check the box at the bottom of the form? Why or why not?

   _____

6. What information goes along the right side of the form? Check all that apply.

   _____ **a.** Date
   _____ **b.** Kind of service desired
   _____ **c.** Charge for shipping
   _____ **d.** Kind of packaging
   _____ **e.** Contents of the package
   _____ **f.** Method of payment
   _____ **g.** Weight

7. Who is paying to ship the package?

   _____

8. Suppose you work for American Home Realty Company at 215 Center Street in Frankfort, KY 40601. The package described above must be sent to Lawrence Rayburn, who works for American Home at 9104 Dayton Avenue in Cincinnati, OH 45202. Complete as much of the form as you can with this information and that above.

Now check the following chart from the delivery service's guide to see how you should send the package.

Skim the chart, and then answer the questions that follow.

SERVICE AND RATES (WITHIN THE CONTINENTAL U.S. AND PUERTO RICO)			
PACKAGING	**WEIGHT AND/OR DIMENSION LIMITS***	**AVAILABLE SERVICE**	**CHARGE**
LETTER	8 oz./9.5" × 12.5" (30 8.5" × 11" sheets)	Next Day A.M. Next Day P.M.	$15.50 $11.50
PACK	12" × 15.5"	Next Day A.M. Next Day P.M.	$15.50 $11.50
BOX	17.5" × 12.5" × 3"	Next Day P.M. Two-Day Three-Day	$13.50 $10.50 $ 7.50
TUBE (triangular)	38" × 6" × 6" × 6"	Next Day P.M. Two-Day Three-Day	$13.50 $10.50 $ 7.50

*FOR GREATER FREIGHTS THAN THOSE LISTED, SEE HEAVYWEIGHT CHART ON PAGE 2 OF SERVICE AND RATE GUIDE.

9. What is the purpose of this chart?

_____

10. What four general kinds of information does the chart give you?

_____

11. Which of these pieces of information do you need to consider when deciding how to send the package? Check all that apply.

_____ a. The recipient of the package
_____ b. The reason you are sending the package
_____ c. The time the package must be received
_____ d. The weight or size of the package
_____ e. Who is paying to send the package

12. What kind of packaging would you use? _____

13. What kind of service would you select? _____

14. Complete the form on the page 50 with this information.

15. How much will the package cost to send? _____

Following Directions

The video program you are about to watch will
show you various forms of instructions you may see
in the workplace. This program will help you read
different types of instructions carefully and follow
them effectively.

As you watch, notice that instructions may appear
in written form or as diagrams or other illustrations.
Note too how important verbal communication is—
sometimes a worker must ask about or talk over
instructions with a co-worker or supervisor.

Think now about how often you follow instructions at
home. Each time you follow a recipe to prepare a new
dish or follow a diagram to install something or put it
together, you are using instructions. Being able to read
and follow instructions is a valuable life skill as well as
work skill.

Sneak Preview

This exercise previews some of the concepts from Program 18. After you answer the questions, use the Feedback on page 55 to help set your learning goals.

CONSTRUCTION: You have a new job in the accounts payable department of a large building contractor. Part of your job is to handle all incoming **invoices** related to ordering electrical, plumbing, and building supplies. To instruct you in this job task, your office manager hands you the **flowchart** below.

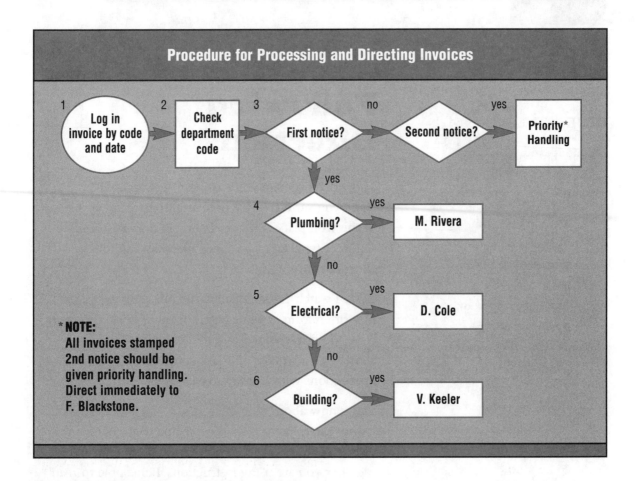

Procedure for Processing and Directing Invoices

1 Log in invoice by code and date → 2 Check department code → 3 First notice? — no → Second notice? — yes → Priority* Handling

3 First notice? — yes ↓

4 Plumbing? — yes → M. Rivera

4 Plumbing? — no ↓

5 Electrical? — yes → D. Cole

5 Electrical? — no ↓

6 Building? — yes → V. Keeler

*NOTE:
All invoices stamped 2nd notice should be given priority handling. Direct immediately to F. Blackstone.

Answer these questions based on the instructions.

1. The purpose, or intended outcome, of these instructions is to have you

   (1) code invoices by department
   (2) send invoices to the correct person for payment
   (3) total how much money the company is being invoiced for
   (4) determine which department owes the most

2. If you open a first invoice for electrical equipment, to whom should it go?

    (1) M. Rivera

    (2) D. Cole

    (3) V. Keeler

    (4) F. Blackstone

3. In your own words, what is priority handling?

_____

_____

4. What might happen if a first-notice plumbing invoice is directed to V. Keeler?

_____

_____

Feedback

- If you got all of the answers right . . .   you have a good foundation for reading written instructions effectively. When you watch the video, pay attention to the various types of written instructions in the workplace.

- If you missed question 1 . . .   focus on skimming to identify the purpose and form—in this case, flowchart—of written instructions.

- If you missed question 2 . . .   pay close attention to reading strategies for understanding instructions, especially step-by-step instructions.

- If you missed question 3 . . .   remember to note special features that further explain instructions.

- If you missed question 4 . . .   look to understand the consequences of what might happen if instructions are not followed.

....

Vocabulary for *Following Directions*

diagram	a drawing or sketch showing how something works or showing a relationship between parts
flowchart	a kind of pictorial instruction that shows the steps in a process or procedure
invoice	a bill for goods or services purchased. Also called a *billing form.*
legend	the explanation of symbols used on a diagram, chart, or map. Sometimes called the *key.*
sequence	a specific order
specifications	a written set of directions or a diagram, sent by a manufacturer, that details how something should be built, installed, or manufactured; called *specs* (pronounced like *specks*) for short
troubleshooting guide	a chart in a product manual that gives options for finding and correcting a problem
visualize	to picture something in one's mind
work orders	written instructions to perform specific job tasks

Now watch Program 18.

After you watch, work on:
• pages 37–52 in this workbook
• Internet activities at www.pbs.org/literacy

AFTER you WATCH

program **18**

Following Directions

On the following pages, you will learn more about the issues discussed in the video program and have an opportunity to develop your skills.

Think About the Key Points from the Video

When you read instructions on the job:
- Skim them first to see what they are explaining.
- Read them carefully.
- Summarize them to make sure you understand.

When you read a **diagram** or other drawing on the job:
- Read and use the key features, such as titles, headings, and legends.
- Look at the diagram carefully.
- Summarize the diagram.

To make sure you can follow instructions:
- Talk or ask about anything you do not understand.
- Be aware of what can happen when instructions are not followed.

WORKTIP

To make sure you understand instructions, you can:
- Restate them to yourself.
- Take notes.
- Explain them to a co-worker.

Reading Written Instructions

Skimming to Identify Forms and Purposes

Workplace instructions may be simply an informal note from a boss or co-worker. Often, however, they are written in the form of memos, manuals, **work orders** to perform a specific job task, or manufacturers' **specifications** that tell how something should be built, installed, or manufactured.

Instructions may be written in paragraphs or in lists. Numbered lists are common when you must follow step-by-step instructions.

Each set of instructions is written for a specific purpose. That means a certain outcome is expected if you follow them. Outcomes for instructions include:

- Doing something.
- Making something.
- Assembling something.
- Fixing something.

By first skimming a set of instructions, you will be able to see what form they are written in—paragraph or list—and what outcome is expected if you follow them.

Skim the instructions from a computer manual below to note their form and purpose.

MAKING LABELS

1. Set the date and code.
   A. Type in the month, day, and year. Press Enter.
   B. Type in your personal ID number. Press Enter.

2. Menu will appear.
   A. Press F1 for label.
   B. Press F2 to check label specifications.
      1. Use Caps Lock key for caps.
      2. Scroll the arrow for type size to set letter size.
   C. Press Esc if specifications are OK.
   D. Press F7 to print.

1. What is the purpose of these instructions?

   _____

2. What form do these instructions take?

   _____

Reading to Understand the Steps

Usually you must do more than one thing to achieve a desired outcome (that is, complete a job task) at work. That is why instructions are often written as a list of steps. Each step must be followed in **sequence**, or order. The steps may be numbered or lettered, or they may begin with clue words such as *first, next, then,* and *finally.*

To understand what you must do, read each step carefully. A good reading strategy is to picture yourself doing each step. Taking brief notes is another good strategy.

Read the instructions for making labels on page 58. Then answer the questions that follow.

1. What is the first thing you do to make a label?

   _____

2. What do you do after the menu appears?

   _____

3. What should you do if you want to use all capital letters for your label?

   _____

Checking Your Understanding by Summarizing

When reading instructions, make sure you understand what to do. The best way to check your understanding is to sum up the instructions in your own words. Restate them to yourself as you read each step, then again after you have read the entire set. Another good way to check your understanding is to explain the instructions to a co-worker. If you find that you do not understand even one step, ask a co-worker or your supervisor.

See if you can number in the correct order these restated steps for making labels.

_____ When the menu appears, press **F1.**

_____ Input your code number.

_____ Input the date.

_____ If it's OK, press **Esc.**

_____ Press **F7** if you want to print the label.

_____ Press **F2** if you want to change any label specifications.

Now try telling a friend or co-worker how to make labels.

Reading Strategies

Read the following directions from a landscaping manual. Pay close attention to the steps to take and the order in which you take them. Then answer the questions that follow.

PREPARING SOIL for a Flower or Vegetable Garden

Many people prepare the soil for gardens by power tilling or digging the grass under. These two methods are incorrect because the grass roots will resprout, and weeds will begin to grow. The correct method of garden preparation is to remove the layer of grass using a garden spade.

First, outline the garden area with a clothesline rope or a hose. Next, apply garden lime along the rope and remove the rope. Then push a spade or edger with your foot all the way around the edge to cut down into the sod. Before you begin removing the sod, make sure garden curves are round and corners are sharp.

To remove the sod, push the spade under a section of the sod just below the grass roots and lift up gently. Sod is heavy and curls, so cut it into manageable sections and roll them up.

To finish, spread compost over the area. You are now ready to turn over the garden soil with a spade or power tiller.

1. What is the outcome of following these instructions?

   (1) a garden planted with vegetables
   (2) a garden planted with flowers
   (3) an area of soil ready to be planted
   (4) a sodded area

2. What do you think Sue might do to help herself understand and remember these instructions?

   (1) begin preparing the soil and go back to these instructions when she runs into a problem
   (2) read the instructions over until she has memorized them
   (3) ask Harry to explain all the instructions to her
   (4) take brief notes of the steps she must follow

3. As Sue read the manual, she decided to rewrite the steps as a numbered list to help her understand and remember them. Rewrite the instructions from the manual as steps in the following numbered list.

To Outline the Garden:	To Remove the Sod:	To Finish the Preparation:
1._____ _____	5._____ _____	7._____ _____
2._____ _____	6._____ _____	8._____ _____
3._____ _____		
4._____ _____		

4. Mr. Chen has instructed that the entire garden be planted with certain flowering plants. Sue makes a sketch of Mr. Chen's yard. The sketch shows that the left side of the garden gets only partial sun, but the right side gets full sun. Harry reminds Sue that the flowering plants Mr. Chen wants require a lot of sun. He asks her to make some recommendations so Mr. Chen's garden will be a success. What changes could Sue recommend to Mr. Chen's instructions for planting flowers?

_____

WRITE IT

Think about something you know how to do well. It can be a household task, a job task, or a hobby. Write instructions for completing the task in step-by-step order. Use additional paper if you need to list more steps.

Directions for _____

STEP 1: _____

STEP 2: _____

STEP 3: _____

STEP 4: _____

Have someone read the directions and tell you if they are clear.

Interpreting Pictorial Instructions

Recognizing Forms of Pictorial Instructions

Workers sometimes have to read instructions in the form of diagrams, maps, or flowcharts. Think of some pictorial instructions—ones that include pictures as well as words—that you have used at home. You may have used diagrams to help you set up a VCR or assemble a child's toy. You have probably used a map to get someplace or to figure out the best bus route to take. On page 130 is a diagram of a common piece of home and office equipment—a computer keyboard.

A flowchart is another kind of pictorial instruction. It guides the reader through a process or a procedure. You follow the arrow to one step, perform a task or make a decision, then follow the appropriate arrow to the next step.

Skim the flowchart below. Then answer the questions that follow.

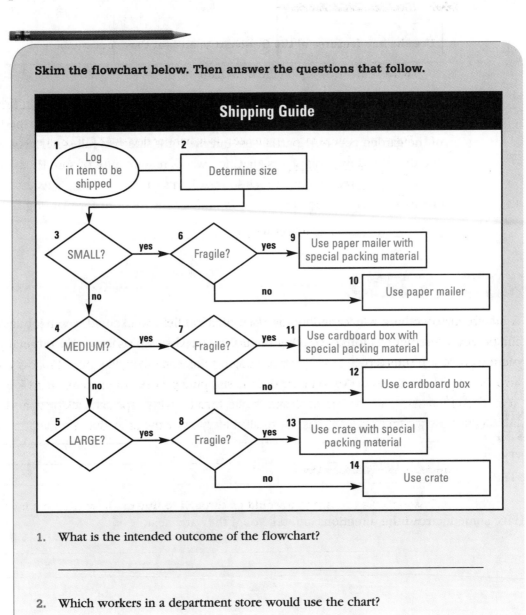

1. What is the intended outcome of the flowchart?

   _____

2. Which workers in a department store would use the chart?

   _____

Using Key Features

Many diagrams, maps, and flowcharts have words along with them, but sometimes this text is only in the form of brief labels or notes. Symbols might also be used. If so, a **legend**, or *key*, lists the symbols and explains them. A good reader and worker uses such key features of pictorial instructions to help understand what to do.

For example, in the case of the flowchart on page 62, numbers indicate order of steps. Shapes drawn around the steps give the worker information about the type of activity:

Oval: Begin   **Diamond:** Make a decision
Rectangle: Do a task   **Arrow:** Go to the next step

Use the key features of the flowchart to answer these questions.

1. What is the first step on the flowchart?

   _____

2. For which things must you make a judgment or decision? Check all that apply.

   _____ **a.** The item to be shipped
   _____ **b.** Its size
   _____ **c.** Its fragility
   _____ **d.** The kind of packaging

Understanding What Is Shown

A picture may be worth a thousand words, but words can help you know if you truly understand the picture. So sum up a diagram or other picture in your own words to see if you "get" the picture. A worker summarizing the flowchart might think something like this: "I follow the arrows and the words *Yes* or *No* to figure out the shipping process for an item. First I log in an item. Then I look at its size. If it is small and fragile, I mail it with a special packing material. If it is not fragile, I use a paper mailer. If it is not small, then I follow the procedure for medium or large."

Describe the process you would go through to find out how to ship a large, non-fragile item.

_____

_____

For more practice in reading a flowchart, see page 131.

RETAIL: Tommy Kim works for a department store. Part of Tommy's job is to arrange the furniture on the display floor of the store.

Problem Solving

Tommy's manager gave him a floor plan—a diagram showing how the furniture is currently arranged. The plan uses picture symbols for the various types of furniture. To read the floor plan, Tommy uses the furniture legend to find out what kind of furniture the symbols stand for. He can then picture where each piece of furniture is positioned on the floor.

Use the diagram below and the legend to answer the questions that follow.

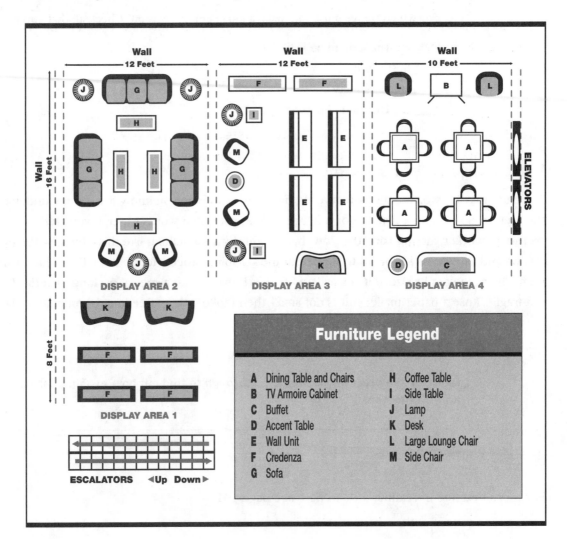

1. Write *True* if the statement is true; *False* if it is false.

    _____ **a.** The furniture floor is on the top level.
    _____ **b.** The furniture floor has display areas of equal size.
    _____ **c.** The furniture floor is approximately 36 ft. by 36 ft.
    _____ **d.** The furniture floor has four display areas.

2. Which type of furniture is on display closest to the elevators?

    _____

3. Which type of furniture is on display in area 2?

    _____

4. If a customer asks Tommy where lamps are displayed, to which area or areas should he direct the customer?

    _____

5. More lounge chairs and side chairs need to be displayed. As a result, most of the credenzas will be moved to the warehouse. From which area will Tommy likely need to move credenzas to make room for the chairs?

    _____

6. **a.** Tommy's manager has told him that there is a problem with the flow of customer traffic through the furniture as it is currently displayed. There is very little browsing through the department. People who get off the elevators cannot see the sofas. What do you think might be the reason for this?

    _____

    b. The manager told Tommy to rearrange the furniture to solve this problem. What might Tommy do to improve the furniture arrangement?

    _____

    _____

COMMUNICATE •

Think about a tool, a small appliance, or some other piece of equipment that you use at home or on the job. Draw a diagram of the item. Label parts. Make a key and tell someone the directions for using the item.

Following Instructions

If you want to achieve a successful outcome, follow the instructions. But for instructions to be followed, they must be clear. *Always read instructions all the way through **before** you start following them.* That way, you will be able to make sure that you understand everything you are supposed to do.

Identifying Unclear Instructions

One way to identify unclear or confusing directions is to **visualize,** or picture, each step before you begin. Ask yourself, "Can I see myself doing what the direction says?"

> Read these instructions from a movie theater employee handbook. They tell ushers how to evacuate patrons in case of fire. See if any part of the instructions is unclear to you.

Evacuation Procedure   **Employee Handbook   20**

1. Have a flashlight and wear an orange jacket.
2. Go to assigned posts: Usher 1 ....Front Center Aisle
                           Usher 2 ....Left Front Exit
                           Usher 3 ....Right Front Exit
                           Usher 4 ....Rear Exit
3. Instruct patrons in first and last rows to file out first.
4. Instruct patrons in second and next to last rows to file out next, etc.
5. Instruct patrons to file out one row at a time.
6. Use flashlights to signal flow of traffic.
7. Assist disabled patrons.

Check each question that you can answer from the instructions above. If the needed information is *not* given in the instructions above, write *CA* for *can't answer.*

_____ 1. Where are the flashlights and orange jackets located?

_____ 2. How do I know who is Usher 1, Usher 2, and so on?

_____ 3. Which patrons should file out first?

_____ 4. Which exit should each row use?

_____ 5. What are flashlights used for?

Getting Clarification

If you are confused by any part of instructions, it is important to get your questions answered before starting to follow them. On the job, you might ask a co-worker or your boss. Sometimes you can clarify instructions by reading on.

Here is a diagram that accompanied the instructions in the theater manual for fire emergency evacuation. Study it to see what it shows.

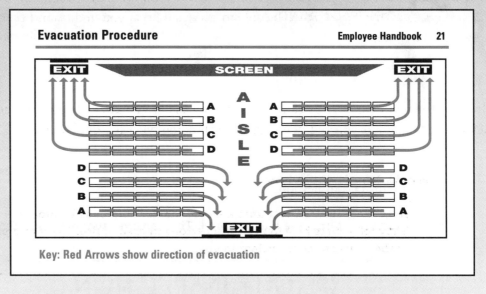

Evacuation Procedure Employee Handbook 21

Key: Red Arrows show direction of evacuation

1. Which particular question from the previous page does this diagram help answer? How?

_____

_____

2. Are there still remaining questions? If you were an usher at the theater, how would you get these questions cleared up?

_____

_____

Understanding the Consequences

When directions are not clear or not entirely understood, mistakes can happen. And mistakes on the job can have many consequences. They can waste time, materials, and money. They can cause dissatisfied co-workers, bosses, and customers. In some cases, following directions can be a matter of health and safety, even a matter of life or death.

Think about the consequences of not clarifying emergency directions before an emergency happens. What might happen?

_____

_____

MANUFACTURING: Ava Morales has just started working for a potato chip company. Part of her new job is to check the weights of bags of chips as they move down the line. She must make sure that the machines are filling the bags with the correct weight of chips.

Following Instructions

As part of Ava's training, her boss has written down the steps she must take to perform this part of her job.

Read the instructions Ava has received. Then answer the questions that follow.

WEIGHT INSPECTION

Recommended procedure is to check four bags at fifteen-minute intervals.

At each inspection interval:

1. Record the time on the inspection chart.

2. Take a bag from the line and place it on the scale.

3. Record its weight on the inspection chart.

4. a. If the weight is 10 ounces give or take 0.5 ounce, replace the bag on the line.
   b. If the weight is more than $\frac{1}{2}$ ounce off, place the bag in the bin.

5. Repeat steps 2–4 for three more bags.

6. If more than one bag must be placed in the bin, halt the line and notify the floor manager and me.

Repeat steps 1–6 at the next inspection interval.

---

1. What is the overall purpose of Ava's instructions?

   (1) to make potato chips

   (2) to fill potato chip bags

   (3) to weigh potato chip bags

   (4) to make sure potato chip bags are filled to the correct weight

2. What should Ava do immediately after she has placed a bag on the scale?

   (1) record its weight
   (2) place it back on the line
   (3) place it in the bin
   (4) weigh three more bags

3. What should Ava do with a bag that weighs 9 ounces?

   _____

4. What should Ava do with a bag that weighs 9.5 ounces?

   _____

5. Ava visualizes herself doing each step. When she reads "halt the line" in step 6, she realizes she does not know how to do that. What should she do?

   _____

6. What might happen if bags are being underfilled and Ava does not follow the directions carefully enough to determine this?

   _____

7. What might happen if bags are being overfilled and Ava does not follow the directions carefully enough to determine this?

   _____

MATH MATTERS ···

Ava's job involves reading a scale and subtracting and adding weights. She needs to know the range of acceptable weights for the potato chip bags. Her boss wrote, "If the weight is 10 ounces give or take 0.5 ounce, replace the bag on the line." You can figure out the range by both subtracting 0.5 from 10 and adding 0.5 to 10:

   10 oz. − 0.5 oz. =

   10 oz. + 0.5 oz. =

Her boss's instructions include both a decimal number (0.5) and a fraction ($\frac{1}{2}$). Ava needs to know that the two numbers are equal, or the same. If you need to be more familiar with decimal and fraction equivalents, use the blank chart on page 126 to list some common ones. A basic math book can help you.

Review

You have seen how skimming workplace instructions—whether written or pictured—can tell you what they are explaining and what the expected outcome is. You have learned strategies such as visualizing, summarizing, and taking notes to help you understand instructions. And you have seen how important verbal communication can be. Sometimes a worker must ask about or talk over instructions with a co-worker or supervisor. This Program Review will give you a chance to show what you have learned.

Imagine that you are printing out a twenty-page list of titles for the video store you work in. But the printer suddenly stops, and the Paper Jam button is lit. To solve the problem, you look for the **troubleshooting guide** in the printer manual, find the section, and see the following instructions.

Skim the instructions below and answer the questions.

Printer Problems

A. If printer stops, check paper supply to see if paper must be added.

B. If printer stops and Paper Jam light is on, follow these directions.
   1. Turn printer off.
   2. Carefully pull out any visible paper that has jammed behind the paper tray. Remove any sheets that are stuck in the output roller.
   3. Open the printer cover. Remove any crumpled paper or small torn pieces that may have stuck to the inside of it.

WARNING: The printer fuser will now be exposed. It is extremely hot. Be careful not to touch the fuser.

   4. Once you have removed all visible paper from inside, follow these steps:
      (1) Lift out the printer cartridge.
      (2) Remove any paper from the feed path.
      (3) Insert the cartridge.
      (4) Close the printer cover.
   5. Reload the paper tray. Carefully fan and align the paper stack in the paper tray.
   6. Turn on the printer and press "Continue." The jammed page will be automatically reprinted.

---

1. How do you know that the instructions listed under B are the ones you need to follow?

   _____

2. Which of the following is the outcome of these instructions?

   (1) You will have to begin the print job all over again.

   (2) The printer will begin the print job where it left off.

3. **a.** How do you know these instructions must be followed step by step?

   _____

   b. Which step has its own set of steps? _____

Read the instructions carefully and answer these questions.

4. What do you do first to clear the paper jam?

   _____

5. What might happen if you don't follow this step in the correct order?

   _____

6. Suppose you do not know what the output roller mentioned in step 2 is. Which of the following things would be a good idea to do? Check all that apply.

   ____ **a.** Just go on to the next step.

   ____ **b.** Look for a diagram in the manual that might explain it.

   ____ **c.** Ask a co-worker or your boss.

   ____ **d.** Look at the printer and guess which part it is.

7. After clearing any paper stuck behind the paper tray and in the output roller, in which two other places should you check to see if there is a paper jam?

   _____

8. What might happen if you touch the fuser?

   _____

9. Number these steps for checking under the printer cartridge in the order in which you should take them.

   ____ Close the cover of the printer.

   ____ Reinsert the printer cartridge.

   ____ Lift out the printer cartridge.

   ____ Remove paper that is jammed in the feed path.

Here are three diagrams from the printer manual. Skim the diagrams and read the text that goes with them. Then answer the questions that follow each one.

To open the printer cover, press the button on the right.

10. What specific information do you learn from this diagram?

_____

11. What step in the instructions on page 70 does this diagram help explain?

_____

To remove the cartridge, gently slide the pins along the grooves on the sides and pull the cartridge toward you.

12. Which step in the instructions on page 70 does this diagram clarify?

_____

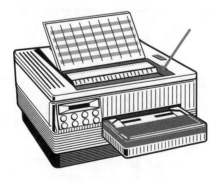

Note the position of the fuser inside the printer. It is labeled Danger: Hot Surface.

13. How can you identify the fuser once the printer is open?

_____

Reading Reports and Manuals

OBJECTIVES

In this lesson, you will work with the following concepts and skills:

1. Understanding the purpose and organization of memos, reports, and references
2. Finding the information you need by skimming, scanning, and using additional sources
3. Using workplace references to complete job tasks and solve problems

In the video program you are about to watch, you will see workers reading memos, reports, and various kinds of workplace reference materials. These references include manuals or handbooks, directories, product specifications, and product information sheets. The program will focus on how to read and use these materials effectively in order to be a success on the job.

As you watch, notice the kind of information each type of reading material gives. Pay special attention to why workers need to read and use each kind of material.

Although the program deals with workplace references, you have probably used similar kinds of references in your own life. A directory is like a phone book. A product information sheet may contain much of the same information as a catalog. And a work manual can be much like a how-to book that explains home repairs or a hobby. Think about other times you have used reference materials, and think of how useful they can be.

Sneak Preview

This exercise previews some of the concepts from Program 19. After you answer the questions, use the Feedback on page 75 to help set your learning goals.

RETAIL: You work for a large hardware store that sells home remodeling supplies. Two customers see kitchen countertops on display and are interested in purchasing a particular kind. Below are parts of a **product information sheet** you can use to answer their questions.

CCC | Chelsea Countertop Company

Standard Laminate Bevel-Edge Countertop

- Top-of-the-line kitchen seller of fine countertops for over 25 years
- Manufactured with microboard to prevent cracking (microboard and laminate expand and contract at the same rate) under standard conditions
- Standard interlock method creates tightest seams and eliminates water penetration under standard conditions
- Plywood used on all installations
- Samples provided ensure proper edge treatment
- One-year warranty on defective materials and workmanship

Size	Price
No backsplash up to $25\frac{1}{2}$" deep	27.95
$25\frac{3}{4}$" to 30" deep	29.95
$30\frac{1}{4}$" to 36" deep	32.95
$36\frac{1}{4}$" to 42" deep	35.95
With 4" backsplash up to $25\frac{1}{2}$" deep	29.95
$25\frac{3}{4}$" to 30" deep	33.95
$30\frac{1}{4}$" to 36" deep	42.95
$36\frac{1}{4}$" to 42" deep	45.95

For custom orders of nonstandard sizes, check in the Appendix.
For ordering and shipping information, see reverse side of page.

Answer these questions based on the product information sheet.

1. What kinds of information does the product information sheet give you? Check all that apply.

    _____ **a.** How the countertops are manufactured

    _____ **b.** How to install the countertops

    _____ **c.** The warranty on the countertops

    _____ **d.** Available sizes

    _____ **e.** Prices

    _____ **f.** Cost of installation

2. The customers are interested in two countertops:

   a. A $25\frac{1}{2}$"-deep countertop with a 4" backsplash
   b. A 32"-deep countertop with a 4" backsplash

   How much would each countertop cost?
   a. _____
   b. _____

3. The customers also need one countertop that is 43 inches deep. Where would you look to find its price?

   _____

4. The customers decide to order the countertops. What would you do now?

   _____

Feedback

If you got all of the answers right . . .	you have a good foundation for reading and using workplace reference materials. When you watch the video, pay attention to the different types of materials there are and the kind of information each gives you.
If you missed question 1 . . .	pay attention to skimming to discover the kind of information a reference material contains.
If you missed question 2 . . .	pay attention to scanning to find the specific information you need.
If you missed question 3 . . .	learn when you need to go to another source for additional information.
If you missed question 4 . . .	focus on how to use information you find to complete a task.

Vocabulary for *Reading Reports and Manuals*

appendix	a section at the back of a book that contains additional related material.
directories	books listing the names and phone numbers of workers in a company or the names, addresses, and phone numbers of companies or groups in a certain industry
glossary	a section at the back of a book that contains special words and their definitions
help screen	a set of instructions on a computer screen that gives step-by-step directions on how to do something on the computer
index	a section at the back of a book that alphabetically lists topics and subtopics covered in the book and the numbers of the pages where they can be found
MSDS	Material Safety Data Sheet; a document from the maker of a hazardous substance that gives instructions on how to use, handle, and dispose of the substance safely
product information sheets	documents listing part of a company's product line, along with product specifications, prices, and ordering and shipping information
product specifications	a particular product's characteristics, including size, weight, color, and uses
reports	documents that give new information about a company's procedures or performance
table of contents	a section at the front of a book listing in order the main parts of the book, including section or chapter titles, and the number of the page on which each begins

PBS

LiteracyLink®

Now watch Program 19.

After you watch, work on:
- pages 77–92 in this workbook
- Internet activities at www.pbs.org/literacy

Reading Reports and Manuals

On the following pages, you will learn more about the issues discussed in the video program and will have an opportunity to develop your skills.

Think About the Key Points from the Video

To be an effective worker, you must become familiar with:

- The different kinds of workplace reading materials.
- What each is used for.
- How each is organized.

To find information in reference materials, you should:

- Skim to see what is inside a reference.
- Scan to find the specific information you need.
- Look in more than one place if you need additional information.

You use references effectively when you:

- Apply their information to complete a job.
- Apply their information to solve problems.
- Think ahead about other information you might need.

Becoming Familiar with Memos, Reports, and Workplace References

Understanding the Purpose

As the video showed, different types of reading materials help workers do their jobs. These materials include memos and **reports** as well as manuals and handbooks, directories, product information sheets, and **product specifications.**

Workers need to read different materials for different purposes. Sometimes a memo is used for a short message or reminder to one person. But it can also be used for important company information that is posted for everyone to see. The memo on page 119 is just such a memo. A report informs you about the company—how it is doing or how it may be changing. Manuals and handbooks, directories, and other references are each used for a specific purpose.

The first step in being able to use these materials effectively is to know what kind of information is in them—in other words, what each is used for. By knowing that, you will know how they can help you succeed in your job.

Match the type of workplace reading material with its purpose.

Type of Material	Purpose
____ 1. Safety manual	a. To send a brief message
____ 2. Directory	b. To explain how to do something safely
____ 3. Employee handbook	c. To detail company benefits
____ 4. Memo	d. To inform about prices, ordering, and shipping
____ 5. Product information sheet	e. To list names and phone numbers
____ 6. Report	f. To explain how to use a product
____ 7. Product specifications	g. To inform about the company's performance

Knowing the Organization

If you know *what kind* of information is in each kind of reading material, you will be able to do your job more effectively and more efficiently. You will not, for example, look in a report when you really need the information that's on a product information sheet. You will be able to do your job even more efficiently if you also know *how* information in each material is organized.

A memo is short and uses a standard format. You can find an example of how a memo is organized on page 119.

A report is longer, sometimes many pages. But it often begins with a brief summary of the information that it contains.

A **directory** is usually a listing of names in alphabetical order.

A manual or handbook is often book length. So it is often organized like a book, with one or more of these sections:

- A **table of contents** appears at the front. It lists the main parts of the book, such as section titles, and the number of the page on which each begins.
- An **index** appears at the back. It is an alphabetical listing of topics and subtopics covered in the book and the numbers of the pages where they can be found.
- A **glossary** appears at the back. It lists and defines special words in alphabetical order.
- An appendix appears at the back. It gives additional related material, such as tables or forms.

Study the table of contents on page 132 and how it is organized. Then answer these questions.

1. How many main content sections does the manual include? _____

2. On what page would you look if you wanted to read about arranging platters? _____

3. Where would you look if you wanted to learn the definition of a catering term?

_____

Study the index on page 132 and how it is organized. Then answer these questions.

4. On what page would you look if you wanted to prepare a baked Alaska? _____

5. On what page would you look if you needed to learn how to staff for a banquet? _____

6. a. On what pages would you look if you were concerned about eliminating bacteria in the kitchen?

_____

   b. Where else could you look?

_____

7. Suppose you looked up *biscuits* but could not find an entry. Under what other topic could you look?

_____

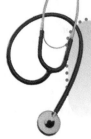

HEALTH CARE: Carl Mann works in a local hospital. He is on break in the staff lounge when he notices a memo on the bulletin board. He goes over to read it.

Reading Strategies

Use each of the following workplace reading materials to answer the questions.

> TO: All Full-Time Employees
> FROM: Human Resources
> RE: Change in Dental Policy
> DATE: March 4
>
> Beginning June 1, Mercy Hospital will include a Dental PPO (Preferred Provider Organization) Plan in its health benefits package. This is in addition to the Dental Insurance now available. Employees who are interested in more information may get a Dental PPO packet from Human Resources as well as a summary sheet comparing the two programs. Open enrollment for the Dental PPO begins May 1.

1. Carl is a full-time nurse attendant at Mercy Hospital. Is the memo intended for him to read? How do you know?

    _____

2. What does the memo concern? How do you know?

    _____

3. Carl thinks he may want to join the Dental PPO. What should he do?

    _____

    The Dental PPO packet contains the following:
    *   *The Dental PPO Handbook*
    *   *Directory of Preferred Providers*
    *   A summary sheet comparing the Dental PPO with the dental insurance offered by the hospital

4. Where should Carl look for a detailed explanation of the benefits and costs of the Dental PPO?

    _____

5. In which part of the packet should he look to see if his current dentist is a preferred provider in the Dental PPO?

_____

Here is the table of contents from *The Dental PPO Handbook.*

6. Carl is especially interested in orthodontic benefits because his ten-year-old daughter needs braces. Where should he look to see what kind of orthodontic procedures are covered?

_____

7. As Carl reads, he comes across the term *habit control appliance.* He is not sure what this refers to. What should he do to find out?

_____

TECH TIP   •••

Computer manuals are essential workplace references. They explain how to use computer programs. In addition, computer menus have a Help option that works something like an index. Choose Help, and an internal menu appears that lists topics. Choose the topic you need help with, and that information then appears on a **help screen.**

Look at the main menu bar on page 123. Read the explanation of how to get to an internal menu. **In what two ways could you get a help screen to appear?**

_____   _____

Finding the Information You Need

Once you are familiar with reference materials in the workplace, you can use them to find information you need to do your job. You are already familiar with skimming and scanning. You can use these approaches to reading reference materials to find information that you need.

Skimming

You know that skimming is passing your eyes quickly over a piece of reading material, picking up main headings and other features, to find out what it contains.

Here is the table of contents from a product guide of a company that manufactures cabinets.

Skim the contents to see what information the guide contains. Then answer these questions.

1. Does the guide contain information on door sizes? _____

2. Does it contain information on optional items? _____

3. Does it appear that you could use this guide to get information on the manufacturer's warranty on the cabinets? _____

Scanning

You know that scanning is quickly looking over a page for key words in order to find specific information.

Scan the table of contents on page 82 to answer these questions.

1. Suppose you were a customer service representative for the cabinet maker. A contractor has asked about ordering cabinets with leaded glass doors. On which sheet would you look?

   _____

2. The contractor needs cabinets that are 44" high. Where would you look to find information you need?

   _____

3. Why would you need to look there?

   _____

Finding All the Information You Need

Sometimes you need to look in different places to get all the information you need. For example, you often must look in a table of contents and sometimes an index just to find the page you should turn to in order to find information. You may also have to use another part of the same book or even another source to get additional information.

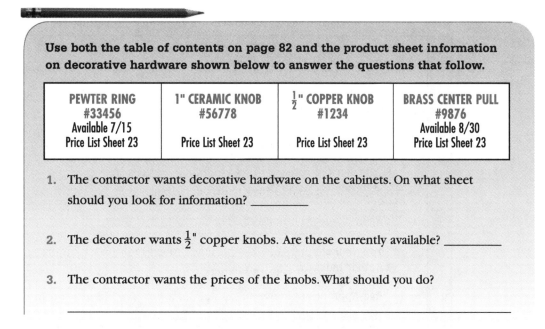

Use both the table of contents on page 82 and the product sheet information on decorative hardware shown below to answer the questions that follow.

PEWTER RING #33456 Available 7/15 Price List Sheet 23	1" CERAMIC KNOB #56778 Price List Sheet 23	$\frac{1}{2}$" COPPER KNOB #1234 Price List Sheet 23	BRASS CENTER PULL #9876 Available 8/30 Price List Sheet 23

1. The contractor wants decorative hardware on the cabinets. On what sheet should you look for information? _____

2. The decorator wants $\frac{1}{2}$" copper knobs. Are these currently available? _____

3. The contractor wants the prices of the knobs. What should you do?

   _____

SERVICE: Choi Bo Wong works for Rainbow World Day Care Center as an aide. The head teacher asks her to produce a list of four or five more books to add to the 3- and 4-year-olds' room.

Decision Making

Read each piece of reference material below to answer the questions.

Choi Bo found five guides on the office shelf:
> *Child Care: A Staff Development Guide*
> *A Directory of Child Care Providers and Funding Organizations*
> *Pivot's Guide to Choosing Books for Children*
> *First Aid*
> *Catalog of Equipment and Supplies for the Child Care Center*

1. Choi Bo skims the titles. Which book should she use?

    _____

2. Which clues could Choi Bo use to make her selection?

    _____

Next Choi Bo skims the table of contents of the book:

Contents

3. How is the main part of the book organized?

_____

4. Where should Choi Bo turn to next?

_____

5. What clue word could she use to decide?

_____

Choi Bo is skimming through the pages of the index organized by ages and sees the following heads:

Infants

Toddlers

Preschoolers

Early Grade

Middle Grades

Young Adults

6. In which section of the index should Choi Bo look for book titles?

_____

Here is part of the index of book titles.

Caps for Sale, 15

Cat in the Hat, The, 140

Corduroy, 23

Curious George, 28

Danny and the Dinosaur, 77

7. On which page should Choi Bo look if she wants to read about the book *Curious George*?

_____

WRITE IT ···

Suppose Choi Bo has selected these four books to order for the 3- and 4-year-olds' room: *Caps for Sale, Curious George, Poems to Read to the Very Young,* and *The Snowy Day.* Which form of written communication should she choose to let the head teacher know: a memo or a report?

If you said memo, you were correct. On another piece of paper, write a memo from Choi Bo to the head teacher, Deletha Morris. Follow the memo format shown on page 119.

Using References Effectively

The information you find in reference materials is there to help you do your job. So if you can use references effectively, you will be a more effective worker.

Completing Jobs

Some jobs simply cannot be done without using a reference. For example, salespersons and customer service representatives must refer to product information sheets and price lists when working with customers. And hotel concierges and travel agents, who make reservations and other arrangements for customers, must refer to directories, guidebooks, and the like.

Below is an activity request form filled out by a hotel concierge. It is now his job to help the guest with his request.

Guest Activity Request

Guest Name _Lewis Young_   Room Number _2110_

Request _Dinner reservations – Greek Islands Restaurant_

Date and Time of Request _10/21 4 p.m._

Date and Time of Activity

    Choice #1 _10/21   6 p.m._

    Choice # 2 _10/21   7 p.m._

Number of people to participate _4_

Arrange transportation?   ☑ Yes   ☐ No

    Type: ☑ Taxi   ☐ House Car   ☐ Limousine   ☐ Rental Car

Request Taken _C. Lewis_

The hotel has a computerized directory for concierges to use. The main menu of that directory has the following options

Medical   **Dental**   **Personal**   **Activities**

The concierge clicks on Activities, and an internal menu appears.

Read the following menu and answer the questions.

TYPE	OPTION	〰 Guest Activities
Sport/Leisure	Fitness Club • Swimming • Massage • Tennis • Bike Rental Racquetball/Handball • Other	
Entertainment	Theater • Comedy • Ballet • Nightclubs • Other	
Dining	Restaurant • Cuisine • Fine Dining	

1. The concierge should scan down to look for which Type of Activity? _____

2. On which Option should he click? _____

Solving Problems

References can also be used when special problems arise. Suppose, for example, that the Greek Islands Restaurant cannot make reservations at the requested times. When the concierge notifies the guest, he responds, "Any good Greek restaurant will do. We just can't eat any later than 7 o'clock. We have theater tickets at 8:30."

Use the Activities menu above to answer these questions.

1. On which Dining Option could the concierge click to find another restaurant that serves Greek food? _____

2. What could the concierge do if he does not understand what the other Dining Options mean?

_____

Thinking Ahead

Going back to a reference can be a waste of time. You can save time and even avoid problems if you think about other information you may need.

Use both the Guest Activity Request form and the guest's response from above to answer this question.

Which of the following information would be good for the concierge to find out as he makes the guest's reservations? Check all that apply.

_____ a. How far the Greek restaurant is from the theater

_____ b. Whether he should arrange for a taxi from the restaurant to the theater

_____ c. What show the guests are going to see

MANUFACTURING: Doug Prosky works for a small machine shop. As part of his job, he must help maintain and clean the equipment. One day, Doug's boss asks him to clean the metal surfaces on which parts are sorted and packed. Doug selects an industrial cleaner from the storeroom.

Problem Solving

Read the product specifications of the cleaning product below and answer the questions.

BRIGHT Aerosol

Active Components: Ammonium Hydroxide, Silicone Dioxide, Isobutane

White foam.

Completely soluble in water.

Boiling point: 200° F.

Uses: Cleans metal and glass surfaces.

Use in normal ventilation.

Normal use does not require breathing mask.

Goggles should be worn to avoid eye contact.

1. Is BRIGHT Aerosol a possible choice for Doug to make to clean the metal sorting surfaces? Why or why not?

   _____

2. List two precautions Doug should take when he uses BRIGHT.

   _____

   _____

As Doug is using the BRIGHT Aerosol, a gust of wind blows through an open window, and the BRIGHT covers his hands. They start to itch and burn. Doug goes to the storeroom to read the **MSDS,** or Material Safety Data Sheet, that the manufacturer of BRIGHT provided. Part of the sheet is shown on the following page.

Skim the safety data sheet below and then answer the questions.

SECTION V	HEALTH HAZARD DATA

EFFECTS OF OVEREXPOSURE

Acute (short-term exposure): Contact with this alkaline mixture may result in irritation to mucous membranes, eyes, and skin. Eye symptoms range from excessive tearing to corneal ulcers and possible blindness. Irritating by inhalation and by mist to upper respiratory tract. Accidental ingestion may cause nausea, diarrhea, and possible perforation of intestinal lining.

Chronic (long-term exposure): Prolonged contact may result in burns or blisters. Exposure to mist may result in chronic inflammation of upper respiratory tract. Ingestion can cause nausea and possible perforation of intestinal lining.

EMERGENCY AND FIRST-AID PROCEDURES

Inhalation: Remove person from area to fresh air. Seek medical attention immediately.

Eye Contact: Object is to seek medical attention immediately. Immediately flush with plenty of water at least 15 minutes, holding eyelids apart to ensure flushing of the entire eye surface.

Skin Contact: Wash with plenty of water. Wash clothing before reuse. If any irritation persists, seek medical attention.

Ingestion: If swallowed, do not induce vomiting. Give large quantities of water. If available, give several glasses of milk. Never give anything by mouth to an unconscious person. Seek medical attention immediately.

3. What should Doug do?

_____

4. Twenty-four hours later, Doug's hands still appear reddish and burn slightly. What should Doug do?

_____

5. In the future, what might Doug do to avoid such a problem again?

   (1) not use BRIGHT aerosol
   (2) use BRIGHT only in unventilated areas
   (3) wear protective gloves
   (4) keep the MSDS binder with him at all times

COMMUNICATE •

Safety is an important issue on any job, and accidents like the one Doug had require a cool head. Discuss with a co-worker, fellow student, family member, or friend the importance of safety. With this partner, try to identify three or four ways to make your workplace, school, or home safer. You may want to identify unsafe conditions and think of possible ways to correct them. You can use the chart on page 126 to list the problems and their solutions.

Review

You have studied memos, reports, manuals, and other kinds of reference materials used in the workplace. You have learned to identify the kinds of information that are in these materials and the ways in which that information is organized. You have seen how to find specific information and how to apply that information to complete a task or solve a problem. This Program Review will give you a chance to show what you have learned.

Suppose you work in a home decorating store that specializes in window treatments and wallpaper. A customer has decided she wants to buy two tassel-trimmed shaped valances to put above two windows with blinds, but the store is out of the brand of valance she wants in the color she wants. You offer to order them from the manufacturer, the Superior Draperies Company.

Use the following parts of the binder that contains the manufacturer's product information sheets to answer the questions.

The binder is divided into sections. The sections have tabs with the following labels:

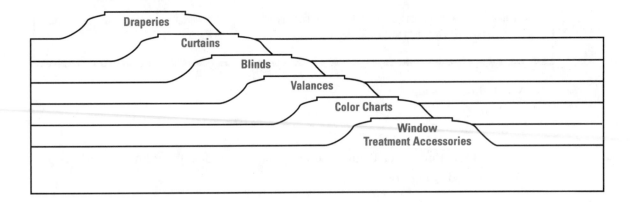

1. Which section should you turn to?

_____

The first page of the section has the following table of contents:

2. To what product information sheet should you turn? _____

On the product information sheet for shaped valances, you find the following information:

Shaped valance
Solid colors only. 86" W × 35" D. (1.6 lb.)
For wide windows, need to use insert valance as well.
840-5955 C   Each 35.00

Tassel-trimmed shaped valance
Rayon fringe.
Solid colors only. 48" W × 30" D. (0.6 lb.)
For wide windows, need to use tassel-trimmed insert valance as well.
Hang on a valance rod using pin hooks.
822-5012 C   Each 28.00

---

3. What stock number should you write down on the order form?_____

4. How much will each valance cost the customer? _____

5. During your store training, you learned that valances should be almost double the width of a window, so that they have a full look when hung. The customer has wide, 40" windows. What else should you tell her she will need to order?

_____

6. To what product information sheet should you now turn? _____

7. According to the product information for tassel-trimmed valances, what else might you suggest to the customer that she may need to buy or order?

_____

8. What section in the product information binder shown on page 90 would you turn to for information on these items?

_____

Suppose one day soon after placing the order, you come into work, and the following memo from the store manager has been posted by the order desk:

MEMO

TO: Sales staff
FROM: Meredith
RE: Orders to Superior Draperies Co.
DATE: 5/3

I've just heard from Superior that there will be lengthy delays in shipping orders because of a fire in their warehouse. Don't place any more orders with them until further notice from me. Also, please notify any customers for whom you may have placed orders that are outstanding. You may be able to find comparable drapes for them with some other manufacturer.

---

9. How do you know that the information in the memo applies to you?

_____

10. What is the first thing you should do?

    (1) wait until you hear from Meredith about the valance order
    (2) tell the customer about the fire when she comes to the store to pick up the valances
    (3) call Superior and ask when it will be able to deliver the valances
    (4) call the customer and tell her about the long delay

11. What should you do next?

    (1) offer to look for similar valances made by another company
    (2) wait for similar valances to be shipped to the store
    (3) wait for the valances to be shipped from Superior
    (4) try to sell valances of another color to the customer

12. Below are some reference materials kept near the order desk. Which might help you solve the problem of the delayed valance order? Check all that apply.

    _____ a. local phone book
    _____ b. *Directory of Drapery Manufacturers*
    _____ c. the product information binder from Superior
    _____ d. product information sheets from other drapery manufacturers
    _____ e. the handbook *Installing Draperies*

Skills Review

On the following pages, you will take a Skills Review. This review will help you find out how well you can now read and use workplace reading materials after having watched the videos and worked through the lessons in this workbook.

Like the preview and the lessons in the workbook, the review consists of real-life materials that workers need to read to do their jobs. These reading materials include memos, forms, charts, instructions, and manuals. After each reading is a set of questions. The questions ask you to show how well you understood the reading and to use the information as a worker would on the job. They may be multiple choice or short answer. For a multiple-choice question, circle the number of the answer you have chosen. For a short-answer question, write on the line provided.

Read each piece of workplace material carefully, and then answer the questions based on it. You may go back and reread to find the answer to a question if you need to.

When you are finished taking the Skills Review, check your answers and complete the evaluation chart. Then compare your results with your results on the Skills Preview. You will see how much you have learned.

Questions 1–6 are based on the following situation.

MANUFACTURING: You have been hired as an inventory clerk for a manufacturer. Inventory clerks are considered hourly workers. Below is part of the employee manual you are given.

Paydays
All salaried employees are paid on the basis of work performed through the two-week period for which the paycheck is issued.

Non-exempt salaried employees are paid for non-standard hours in the following pay period.

Hourly employees are paid on a weekly basis for the hours worked the previous week.

Time Cards for Hourly Workers
The time clock is located between the men's and women's locker rooms.

Punch in at the beginning of your shift and out at the end. You may not punch in more than 15 minutes before your shift. One-half hour for lunch is automatically deducted from your time each day, so do not punch in or out for lunch. If you leave the grounds for personal business, you must punch in and out.

Time Sheets for Non-exempt Salaried Workers
Time sheets must be completed every day and turned in to your supervisor for approval every two weeks. Include late arrivals, early departures, and absences for personal business, approved or otherwise.

Overtime Pay
All hourly workers are eligible for overtime pay at the rate of $1\frac{1}{2}$ times their regular hourly rate for all hours worked in excess of 40 hours in one week.

All non-exempt salaried workers receive overtime pay at the rate of $1\frac{1}{2}$ times their regular hourly rate for all hours worked in excess of 40 hours in one week.

Holidays, vacation days, and sick days are not credited as hours worked toward computing overtime.

---

1. The purpose of this page is to

   (1) inform you of payroll procedures
   (2) explain how to punch a time clock
   (3) train you how to do your job
   (4) explain company holidays

2. What is the main idea of the page?

   (1) All salaried employees are paid for two-week periods.
   (2) The company does pay overtime pay to some of its employees.
   (3) Holidays, vacation days, and sick days are not credited toward overtime.
   (4) There is a distinction in payroll procedures between hourly and salaried workers.

3. How often will you be paid as an inventory clerk?

   _____

4. How do you notify the company of the time you spend working?

   _____

5. Are you eligible for overtime pay? Why or why not?

   _____

6. Which of the following would *not* be an example of leaving the grounds for "personal business"?

   (1) going to the dentist with an emergency toothache
   (2) picking up your sick child at school
   (3) dropping off a company package at an express delivery box
   (4) going out for an hour-long lunch

Questions 7 and 8 are based on the following information.

Part of your job as inventory clerk is to record information from material certification forms that must accompany each shipment you log in. Here is one such form.

MATERIAL CERTIFICATION

This is to certify that the material used in the manufacturing of your:

PART/PRODUCT NO. _122-674_   PURCHASE ORDER NO. _M6778_

DESCRIPTION: _Internal Threaded Bushing_   QUANTITY PROVIDED: _3,500 units_

was Virgin Nytrel (per your specifications) in $1\frac{1}{2}$" diameter rods, as provided to Nixon Nails from its supplier, CDE Enterprises.

---

7. What is the purpose of this form?

   _____

8. What would you record as the number of internal threaded bushings shipped to your company? _____

Questions 9–13 are based on the following situation.

SERVICE: Bonita Drew is a customer service representative for a clothes catalog house. She is taking a phone order from a customer. Below is the order form as she has completed it so far.

Sold To:			Ship To:		
Angela Pons 219 Eastern Ave. Forest Lake, IL 60699			Same		

Order #		Order Date		Order Taker	
P132091		9/13		Bonita Drew	

Catalog No.	Description	Size/Color	Quantity	Price	Total
4407200	Denim jacket	Medium/ Blue	1	$45.00	$45.00
4432200	Turtleneck sweater	Medium/ Yellow	1	$20.00	$20.00

Credit Card Number _____

Exp. Date _____

Subtotal $65.00

Shipping/Handling   _____

SalesTax (if applicable)   _____

TOTAL   _____

9. Who is placing an order for clothes?

_____

10. Who is taking the order?

_____

11. What address should the clothes be shipped to?

_____

_____

12. What kind of information must be recorded in the bottom left-hand corner of the form?

_____

13. What does Exp. Date mean?

_____

Questions 14–16 are based on the following chart. Use the chart to determine the shipping and handling charges for the order on page 96.

SHIPPING & HANDLING

The following amount must be added to the order for each delivery address. For shipment outside the contiguous U.S., including Alaska and Hawaii, use Chart B. For Rush delivery, see also Chart C.

If total is	Add
$19.99 or less	$ 4.95
20.00–29.99	5.95
30.00–39.99	6.95
40.00–49.99	7.95
50.00–74.99	8.95
75.00–99.99	10.95
100.00–149.99	13.95
150.00 or more	15.95

14. What shipping and handling charge should be added to the order?

_____

15. What might happen if the wrong address is recorded?

_____

16. What might happen if you forget to fill in the credit card number?

_____

Questions 17–23 are based on the following situation.

CONSTRUCTION: You work as an installer for a large hardware store and are installing a new brand of bathtub wallboard. You have already followed the instructions to remove the faucets and tub spout from the wall and measured and cut the wallboard panels to fit. Now you are ready to install the panels. Here is the final set of instructions.

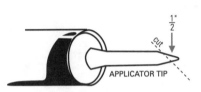

Figure 1. Adhesive Applicator

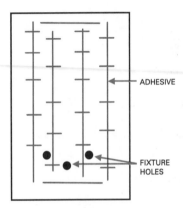

Figure 2. Fixture Panel

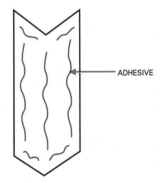

Figure 3. Corner Panel

Installing the Tub Wallboard

1. Make sure wall surface and back surface of wallboard are clean and dry.

2. Cut nozzle tip of the adhesive applicator as shown in **Figure 1.** This will apply a $\frac{1}{8}$" bead of adhesive. If you apply any larger bead, the adhesive will show through the panels. You may need to push a nail into the tip of the applicator to get the adhesive flowing.

3. Apply adhesive to the panel for the fixture wall as shown in **Figure 2.** Be sure to keep the adhesive bead well away from all panel edges. Leave about a 1" space from panel edge. The finishing caulk must not come in contact with the adhesive.

4. Install the panel on the fixture wall. Press firmly into place.

5. Install the opposite end panel the same way.

6. Install the back wall panel as measured and marked in the same way.

7. Apply adhesive to a corner panel as shown in **Figure 3.** Install into corner of fixture wall and back wall as measured and marked.

8. Install the opposite corner in the same way.

9. Use caulk to seal all panel edges, around fixtures, and around the top of the tub.

10. Reinstall faucets and tub spout.

17. Why do you think the wall and back of the wallboard must be clean and dry before you apply the adhesive?

_____

18. How far back from the tip should you cut the adhesive applicator?

_____

19. What might happen if you cut the hole larger than what is shown in **Figure 1**?

   (1) The adhesive will not hold.
   (2) A nail will be needed to get the adhesive flowing.
   (3) Too much adhesive will come out and show through.
   (4) The adhesive will not flow smoothly.

20. Picture yourself installing each of the five wall panels. Number each panel below in the order in which you would install it.

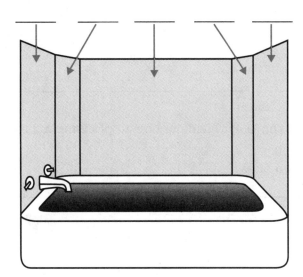

21. What is the next step after you install the final panel?

_____

22. What might happen if you apply the adhesive too close to the panel edges?

_____

23. Which of the following questions is not answered by the instructions?

   (1) How large should the adhesive bead be?
   (2) What do you do after you have installed the fixture panel?
   (3) Where do you apply caulk?
   (4) What can happen if the caulk comes in contact with the adhesive?

Questions 24–30 are based on the following situation.

RETAIL: You are a receptionist in a company that imports TV and other electronic parts made in Mexico. Your boss must talk to the head of a company in Mexicali, Mexico. He asks you to place the call for him. You have the local number of the company, but you have never placed an international phone call before. So you look in the beginning of the phone book for information.

CONTENTS

---

24. On what page would you look to find out how to place the call to Mexico? _____

Here is the information you find.

MAKING A DIRECT-DIAL CALL

- International Access Code (011) + Country Code + City Code (if any) + Number
- Wait at least 45 seconds for ring.
- See Selected Country and City Code chart below. For codes not listed, call your long-distance company.

MAKING AN OPERATOR-ASSISTED CALL

- Call your chosen long-distance company for instructions on how to make a person-to-person, collect, calling card, or third-number call.

---

25. What information might you have asked your boss for in advance?

(1) if he wants you to call direct or through an operator

(2) what your chosen long-distance company is

(3) what the international access code is

(4) if Mexicali has a city code

26. How would you make a person-to-person call?

_____

27. What two numbers must you still find in order to dial the company direct?

_____

Here is a portion of the code chart.

Location	Code	Location	Code	Location	Code	Location	Code
Algeria	21	Czech Republic	42	Hong Kong	853	Kuwait*	965
American Samoa*	648	Prague	2	Hong Kong	5	Lesotho	266
Andorra	376	Denmark	45	Kowloon	3	Liberia*	231
All points	628	Aalborg	8	Hungary	136	Libya	21
Argentina	54	Copenhagen	1 or 2	Budapest	1	Libya	21
Buenos Aires	1	Ecuador	593	Iceland	354	Liechtenstein	41
Cordoba	51	Guayaquil	4	Reykjavik	1	All points	75
Aruba	297	Quito	2	India	91	Luxembourg*	352
Ascension Island*	247	Egypt	20	Bombay	22	Macau*	853
Australia	61	Alexandria	3	Calcutta	33	Malawi*	265
Melbourne	3	Cairo	2	New Delhi	11	Malaysia	60
Sydney	2	El Salvador*	503	Indonesia	62	Kuala Lumpur	3
Austria	43	Ethiopia	251	Jakarta	21	Malta	356
Innsbruck	5222	Addis Ababa	1	**INMARSAT**		Marshall Islands	692
Vienna	1	Faeroe Islands	298	Atlantic Ocean	871	Mexico	52
Bahrain*	973	Fiji*	679	Pacific Ocean	872	Mexicali	656
Bangladesh*	880	Finland	358	Indian Ocean	873	Mexico City	5
Belgium	32	Helsinki	0	Atlantic Ocean West	874	Tijuana	66
Antwerp	3						691
Brussels	2		33	Iran			77

28. What is the country code for Mexico? _____

29. What is the city code for Mexicali? _____

30. What would you do if the number for Mexicali was not listed on the chart?

    (1) tell your boss you cannot place the call

    (2) assume the city has no code

    (3) dial your long-distance company to ask

    (4) dial the operator to ask

Skills Review Answer Key

1. (1) inform you of payroll procedures
2. (4) There is a distinction in payroll procedures between hourly and salaried workers.
3. every week
4. by punching in and out with a time card
5. yes, because all hourly workers are eligible, and you are an hourly worker
6. (3) dropping off a company package at an express delivery box
7. to notify your company what material was used to make its bushings
8. 3,500 units
9. Angela Pons
10. Bonita Drew
11. 219 Eastern Ave.
    Forest Lake, IL 60699
12. information about payment by credit card
13. expiration date, the date until which the credit card can be used
14. $8.95
15. The shipment will be sent to the wrong person.
16. Bonita will have to contact Ms. Pons again. Her order will be delayed.
17. The adhesive won't hold well if applied to a dirty surface.
18. $\frac{1}{2}$"
19. (3) Too much adhesive will come out and show through.
20. 1, 4, 3, 5, 2
21. Use caulk to seal the panel edges, around the fixtures, and around the top of the tub.
22. It might spread to the edge and come in contact with the caulk.
23. (4) What can happen if the caulk comes in contact with the adhesive?
24. page 7
25. (1) if he wants you to call direct or through an operator
26. call the long-distance company your company has chosen
27. the country code and city code
28. 52
29. 656
30. (3) dial your long-distance company to ask

Skills Review Evaluation Chart

This chart will help you recognize the skills you do well. Circle the question numbers that you answered correctly. Then fill in the number of questions you got correct for each program lesson. Find the total number correct, and review the lessons you had trouble with.

Program Lesson	Question Number	Number Correct/Total
16: *Reading for a Purpose* Reading for Different Purposes, Using Different Approaches to Reading, Using Strategies to Understand What You Read	1, 2, 3, 4, 5, 6, 7, 8	___/8
17: *Finding What You Need: Forms and Charts* Understanding Forms, Understanding Charts, Using Forms and Charts	9, 10, 11, 12, 13, 14, 15, 16	___/8
18: *Following Directions* Reading Written Instructions, Interpreting Pictorial Instructions, Following Instructions	17, 18, 19, 20, 21, 22, 23	___/7
19: *Reading Reports and Manuals* Becoming Familiar with Memos, Reports, and Workplace References; Finding the Information You Need; Using References Effectively	24, 25, 26, 27, 28, 29, 30	___/7
	Total	___/30

Turn to page 104 to see what your score means.

If you got 27–30 correct: You have strong reading skills and a good understanding of how to effectively apply those skills on the job.

If you got 24–26 correct: Try to figure out why you got each answer wrong. Review the sections for the items you missed to improve your reading of workplace materials.

If you got 21–23 correct: You need to improve your workplace reading skills. Review any program in which you missed more than one item.

If you got less than 21 correct: You need to review the basic reading skills in each program. By reviewing the programs and revisiting the exercises in this book, you can gain the knowledge and skills you need to be effective when reading workplace materials.

Answer Key

Understanding the Purpose of Reading Materials, page 18

1. (3)
2. (1)

Understanding Your Purpose for Reading, page 19

Sample answers:

1. to find out Tri-Tech's attendance policy
2. attendance policy
3. Procedures must be followed for tardiness.
4. Absences must be approved.
5. The company has an attendance policy that is strictly enforced.

WorkSkills, pages 20–21

1. to learn how to run the daily check on the Health and Safety stations
2. the Health and Safety stations at Northern Bay Hospital
3. Sample answer: Eye wash stations are well marked and located in each wing, the kitchen, and laundry. EPE stations are clearly marked and located in each wing and contain certain essential protective equipment.
4. Sample answer: He should carry the policy with him as he checks each station. He also might want to make a checklist based on the policy to carry with him.
5. Sample answer: He should notify his boss of the problems.

Write It, page 21

Sample answer:

To: Amy Anderson
Topic: Health and Safety Station Check

I've discovered the following two safety problems:

- The E Wing EPE station is low on medium-sized gloves.
- A piece of kitchen equipment is partially blocking the sign and access to the eye wash station in the kitchen.

Please advise me on solving these problems.

Adjusting Your Speed, page 22

1. Q
2. S
3. S
4. Q

Skimming, pages 22–23

1. patients' diets
2. Room and Bed Number, Name, Kind of Diet
3. bed 1 or bed 2 in each room

Scanning, page 23

1. Scott Penny
2. Jasmine Allen
3. three
4. no
5. before you are employed (pre-employment), upon reasonable suspicion by a manager or co-worker, and after an accident or near accident

WorkSkills, pages 24–25

1. Pay Stub, Pay Stub Key, and Pay Stub Codes
2. payments (income)
3. Federal Income Tax
4. $750.00
5. $150.00
6. FIT (Federal Income Tax) $132.00; FICA (Social Security Tax) $66.00; Medical/Dental Insurance ($12.05)
7. retroactive pay adjustments for the year to date

Developing Comprehension Strategies, page 26

1. to learn the hand-to-counter method of counting out money
2. your left hand
3. Sample answer: First, tell someone, "To use the hand-to-counter method, hold the money, highest bills on top, in the hand you don't write with. Pass the bills from that hand to the opposite hand and then to a pile on the counter. Count as each bill is passed. Put each bill down, but make sure you look for worn, torn, or counterfeit bills as each bill is passed." Then demonstrate the procedure.

Developing Vocabulary Strategies, page 27

Answers may vary; suggested answers:

1. the direction or line in which fibers in a fabric run

2. a finished edge that will not fray

3. a stitched fold of fabric

4. an allowance or difference in measure between the sewing line and cutting line

WorkSkills, pages 28–29

1. to learn how to use a forklift safely

2. how to pick up a load, how to drive with a load, and how to set down a load

3. a. Sample answer: Make sure nothing is blocking your vision in any direction.

   b. Sample answer: Position the forklift so that you approach the load straight on, not from an angle.

4. (2)

5. a. a support pole

   b. to make stable; to make sure something will not fall or tumble

   c. anything that can block the forklift's path or get in its way

Review, pages 30–32

1. (1)

2. automotive training courses, qualifications for the course program, and how to register

3. jobs, descriptions, qualifications, and training courses

4. fairly quickly, because you just want to learn the main idea of the notice and the key details

5. (2)

6. A mechanic handles routine maintenance tasks, while a technician does specialized tasks.

7. a. False

   b. True

   c. True

   d. False

   e. False

   f. True

8. a and c

9. a. tune-up technician

   b. Tune-up Basics and Advanced Tune-up

10. a. mechanic

    b. Basic Auto Mechanics I and II

PROGRAM 17: FINDING WHAT YOU NEED: FORMS AND CHARTS

Reviewing Common Forms, page 38

1. (3)

2. a postal worker

Identifying Workplace Forms, page 39

1. c

2. e

3. b

4. d

5. a

Reading a Form, page 39

2, 4, 5

WorkSkills, pages 40–41

1. to state what hours and days an employee is available to work

2. a, c, d

3. Monday, August 20

4. Thursday and Friday

5. 40 for the first week, 32 for the second

6. yes, because the supervisor signed the form

7. See answers below.

DO: Day off	V: Vacation Day	H: Holiday	P: Personal Day					
Mon 9/10	Tues 9/11	Wed 9/12	Thur 9/13	Fri 9/14	Sat 9/15	Sun 9/16		
Hrs 8	8	8	DO	DO	8	8	Total	40
Mon 9/17	Tues 9/18	Wed 9/19	Thur 9/20	Fri 9/21	Sat 9/22	Sun 9/23		
Hrs 8	8	8	8	P	DO	DO	Total	32

Reviewing Common Charts, page 42

1. False

2. False

3. True

4. True

Recognizing Workplace Charts, pages 42–43

1. to show the hours that each assistant manager is working

2. Sample answers: so that employees know when they are working and when others are working; so that the manager can make sure an assistant manager will always be on duty

Reading a Chart, page 43

1. 6:30 A.M. to 3:30 P.M.

2. Alonzo

3. Chris; otherwise Alonzo would have to work 6:30 A.M.–12:00 A.M.

WorkSkills, pages 44–45

1. Tuesday breakfast

2. eggs

3. orange juice

4. a. one slice of diet wheat bread

   b. ask a co-worker or her boss

5. 1 cup of 2% milk, a 4- to 6-ounce glass of orange juice, 1 cup of cold cereal, 1 bran muffin, 1 slice of diet wheat bread, and 1 scrambled egg

6. the low cholesterol diet; because egg yolks and 2% (or non-skim) milk are higher in cholesterol

7. Sample answer: The 1,200-calorie meal plan has 800 fewer calories than the 2,000-calorie meal plan. In the 2,000-calorie plan, either the foods have more calories (for example, a bran muffin instead of a diet bran muffin), or a larger amount is allowed (for example, 8 ounces of orange juice instead of just 4).

8. a. True

   b. True

   c. False

   d. False

Completing Forms and Charts, page 46

Tenant's Name: Dwight Small

Apt.: 4F

Problem Description: Air conditioner doesn't work; water leaking from it

Priority 2 (handle in 24 hours)

Answer Key   107

Interpreting Information, page 46

1. by 6:30 P.M. on 7/6
2. Action Taken: valve replaced

    Date/Time Resolved: 11 A.M. 7/6

    Hours Spent: $\frac{1}{2}$ hr.
3. Dwight Small, the tenant, and Dave Gray, Bill's supervisor, both need to initial the form.

Understanding the Importance of Accuracy, page 47

1. Sample answer: Bill Smoltz may not go immediately to the correct apartment; or it might take some time before he locates the correct one. Also, Dwight Small's baby may suffer from the heat, and the tenant-landlord relationship might be hurt.
2. Sample answer: Dave Gray might need to contact Dwight Small to make sure he is satisfied that the air conditioner is fixed.

WorkSkills, pages 48–49

1. 3492
2. 30
3. the total cost for each title; his signature
4. 1-319-555-7777
5. (2)

Tech Tip, page 49

1. Title
2. In Stock

Review, pages 50–52

1. to give information about where and how to ship a package
2. (1)
3. (2)
4. (3)
5. No. Because the package needs to get there the next day, Thursday.
6. b, d, f, g
7. the sender (your office)
8. See answers below.
9. to list the kinds of shipping services and rates a delivery company offers
10. types of packaging, weight and/or dimension limits, available services, and charges
11. c and d
12. Pack
13. Next Day A.M.
14. See form with answer to question 8.
15. $15.50

SHIPPING LABEL

FROM:

Date *(Date)*   Internal Reference No. *C21*

Name *(Your Name)*

Company   American Home Realty Company

Address   215 Center St.

City   Frankfort   State   KY   ZIP Code   40601

TO:

Name   Lawrence Rayburn

Company   American Home Realty Company

Address   9104 Dayton Ave.

City   Cincinnati   State   OH   ZIP Code   45202

For Saturday Delivery, check here ☐

Signature   *(Your signature)*

PACKAGE SERVICE

Next Day A.M.	Next Day P.M.	Two-Day
☑	☐	☐

FREIGHT SERVICE

Next Day	Two-Day	Three-Day
☐	☐	☐

PACKAGING

Letter ☐   Box ☐
Pack ☑   Tube ☐

PAYMENT Bill to:
Sender ☑
Recipient ☐
Third Party ☐

Account No.
549-02-371

Credit Card No.

Total Packages   1

Total Weight

PROGRAM 18: FOLLOWING DIRECTIONS

Skimming to Identify Forms and Purposes, page 58

1. to explain how to make labels
2. a step-by-step list, numbered and lettered. (You may have recognized this kind of list as being an outline.)

Reading to Understand the Steps, page 59

1. Set the date and code.
2. Press F1 for label.
3. Use the Caps Lock key.

Checking Your Understanding by Summarizing, page 59

3, 2, 1, 5, 6, 4

WorkSkills, pages 60–61

1. (3)
2. (4)
3. **To Outline the Garden:**

   1. Outline garden area with rope or hose.
   2. Apply garden lime along rope and remove it.
   3. Push spade into sod around edge.
   4. Make sure garden curves are round and corners are sharp.

   To Remove the Sod:

   5. Push spade under sod below roots and lift gently.
   6. Cut sod into manageable sections and roll up.

   To Finish the Preparation:

   7. Spread compost over area.
   8. Turn over soil.
4. Possible answer: plant flowering plants that require only partial sun on the left side of the garden

Recognizing Forms of Pictorial Instructions, page 62

1. to help the user choose the correct packaging for shipping specific types of items
2. those working in the shipping department

Using Key Features, page 63

1. Log in the item to be shipped.
2. b and c

Understanding What Is Shown, page 63

Sample answer: First I'd log in the item. Then I'd look at it and figure it was large but not fragile. The flowchart tells me to ship it in a crate.

WorkSkills, pages 64–65

1. a. False
   b. False
   c. False
   d. True
2. dining tables and chairs
3. living room furniture (sofas, side chairs, lamps, and coffee tables)
4. areas 2 and 3
5. area 1
6. a. The wall units in display area 3 block their view.
   b. Possible answer: Move the wall units back against the walls in area 2 and the sofas to area 3.

Identifying Unclear Instructions, page 66

1. CA
2. CA
3. ✓
4. CA
5. ✓

Getting Clarification, pages 66–67

1. Which exit should each row use? The diagram uses arrows to point from rows to exits.
2. Yes. Possible answer: I would first read all of the instructions. Then I would ask the head usher or manager.

Understanding the Consequences, page 67

Possible answer: During an emergency, it may be too late to find out what you should do. Someone could get injured or killed.

WorkSkills, pages 68–69

1. (4)
2. (1)
3. put it in the bin
4. put it back on the line
5. ask her boss
6. Possible answer: Customers might notice and complain.
7. Possible answer: Over the long term, the company would make less money.

Math Matters, page 69

10 oz. − 0.5 oz. = 9.5 oz.
10 oz. + 0.5 oz. = 10.5 oz.
Some common fraction-decimal equivalents are $\frac{3}{4}$ = 0.75, $\frac{1}{2}$ = 0.5, $\frac{1}{4}$ = 0.25, and $\frac{1}{5}$ = 0.2.

Review, pages 70–72

1. because the Paper Jam button is lit
2. (2)
3. a. because they are numbered
   b. step 4
4. Turn the printer off.
5. Possible answers: You might get a shock. The machine might start again before you're ready and injure you.
6. b and c
7. under the printer cover and in the feed path
8. You might get burned.
9. 4, 3, 1, 2
10. how to open the printer cover
11. step B-3
12. step B = 4 (1)
13. It is labeled Danger: Hot Surface.

PROGRAM 19: READING REPORTS AND MANUALS

Understanding the Purpose, page 78

1. b
2. e
3. c
4. a
5. d
6. g
7. f

Knowing the Organization, pages 78–79

1. 5
2. page 35
3. the Glossary of Catering Terms, beginning on page 48
4. page 158
5. page 253
6. a. pages 70, 192, 193, 276
   b. in the Index under both Food-Borne Illnesses and Sanitation
7. Breads

WorkSkills, pages 80–81

1. Yes. Because it is directed to all full-time employees.
2. A change in the dental policy. That topic is listed after *Re:*.
3. He should go to Human Resources and get a Dental PPO packet and a comparison summary sheet to study.
4. *The Dental PPO Handbook*
5. *Directory of Preferred Providers*
6. page 4
7. look in the Glossary, beginning on page 9

Tech Tip, page 81

click on Help and then the topic you need help with; press the alt key and type H, then click on the topic you need help with

Skimming, page 82

1. yes
2. yes
3. It does not appear so from the table of contents.

Scanning, page 83

1. sheet 5
2. Custom Sizes, sheet 9
3. because 44" is not a standard size offered by the company

Finding All the Information You Need, page 83

1. sheet 12
2. yes
3. look at price list sheet 23

WorkSkills, pages 84–85

1. *Pivot's Guide to Choosing Books for Children*
2. the words *Books* and *Children*
3. by kind of book
4. Age-Appropriate Indexes, beginning on page 265
5. Age
6. Preschoolers
7. page 28

Write It, page 85

Sample memo:

TO: Deletha Morris
FROM: Choi Bo Wong
RE: Books for 3- and 4-year-olds
DATE: (Today's Date)

I've studied *Pivot's Guide to Choosing Books for Children* and decided these four books would be good to add to the preschoolers' library: *Caps for Sale, Curious George, Poems to Read to the Very Young,* and *The Snowy Day.* We can discuss this when you have time.

Completing Jobs, pages 86–87

1. Dining
2. Restaurant

Solving Problems, page 87

1. Cuisine
2. Possible answers: (1) ask a co-worker, (2) click on each one and try to determine what it refers to by what's listed on the next screen, or (3) use a Help screen if one is on the menu

Thinking Ahead, page 87

1. a and b

WorkSkills, pages 88–89

1. yes, because the specifications say it cleans metal surfaces
2. Make sure there is normal ventilation. Wear goggles.
3. Wash his hands with plenty of water. If any got on his clothes, he should wash them too.
4. Go to a doctor.
5. (3)

Review, pages 90–92

1. Valances
2. 6
3. 822-5012 C
4. $28.00
5. two tassel-trimmed insert valances
6. 4
7. valance rods and pin hooks
8. Window Treatment Accessories
9. because you are a member of the sales staff and you dealt with Superior Draperies recently
10. (4)
11. (1)
12. b and d

Glossary

appendix: a section at the back of a book that contains additional related material

attendance policy: a company's written plan and procedures for handling employee attendance

context clues: hints about the meaning of a word found in the surrounding words in the sentence or paragraph

database: a collection of information that can be organized in different ways

diagram: a drawing or sketch showing how something works or showing a relationship between parts

directories: books listing the names and phone numbers of workers in a company or the names, addresses, and phone numbers of companies or groups in a certain industry

e-mail: written communication sent by computer; short for *electronic mail*

field: an area in a computerized form, sometimes appearing as a colored box, which requires a specific piece of information

flowchart: a kind of pictorial instruction that shows the steps in a process or procedure

glossary: a section at the back of a book that contains special words and their definitions

help screen: a set of instructions on a computer screen that gives step-by-step directions on how to do something on the computer

icon: a small picture on a computer screen that stands for a program or command

index: a section at the back of a book that alphabetically lists topics and subtopics covered in the book and the numbers of the pages where they can be found

inventory: an itemized list of the goods that a store or business currently has in stock

invoice: a bill for goods or services purchased. Also called a *billing form.*

keyboard: the part of a computer with letters, numbers, and function keys for inputting information

legend: the explanation of symbols used on a diagram, chart, or map. Sometimes called the key.

main idea: the most important point a writer is making

manual: a small reference book, giving training on how to do something or information about a company and its policies. Sometimes called a *handbook.*

memo: a written communication in a business office; short for *memorandum*

menu: a list that appears on a computer screen from which the user can choose a program, command, or file

monitor: the part of a computer with a screen that displays stored information

MSDS: Material Safety Data Sheet; a document from the maker of a hazardous substance that gives instructions on how to use, handle, and dispose of the substance safely

paycheck stub: a table that accompanies a paycheck and details income and deductions

product information sheets: documents listing part of a company's product line, along with product specifications, prices, and ordering and shipping information

product specifications: a particular product's characteristics, including size, weight, color, and uses

purchase order: a form used to list one or more items to buy

reports: documents that give new information about a company's procedures or performance

resource: anything a person can use—a book, person, computer—to get needed information

safety policy: a company's written plan and guidelines for employee safety

scan: to move the eyes over a page of reading material, looking for key words or phrases, in order to locate specific information. To scan a chart or diagram, use column and row headings, labels, or keys to help locate information.

sequence: a specific order

skim: to quickly read over any titles, headings, and pictures or charts that are included in a piece of reading material, in order to get a sense of what it is about

specifications: a written set of directions or a diagram, sent by a manufacturer, that details how something should be built, installed, or manufactured; called *specs* (pronounced like *specks*) for short

strategies: methods a person can use to better understand what he or she reads

table of contents: a section at the front of a book listing in order the main parts of the book, including section or chapter titles, and the number of the page on which each begins

troubleshooter: a worker who locates problems and solves them

troubleshooting guide: a chart in a product manual that gives options for finding and correcting a problem

visualize: to picture something in one's mind

work orders: written instructions to perform a specific job task

work schedules: charts showing employees' assigned work hours

Index

REFERENCE HANDBOOK

Reading a Memo

A memo, or memorandum, is a form of written communication used by most companies. A memo can be from one person to another or from one person to a group of people, a department, or even a whole company. Memos are often used by managers and supervisors to inform workers about an important issue. They are usually short and to the point. A memo can usually be read fairly quickly for the main idea and key details.

Memos follow a standard format so readers can quickly find out the following information:

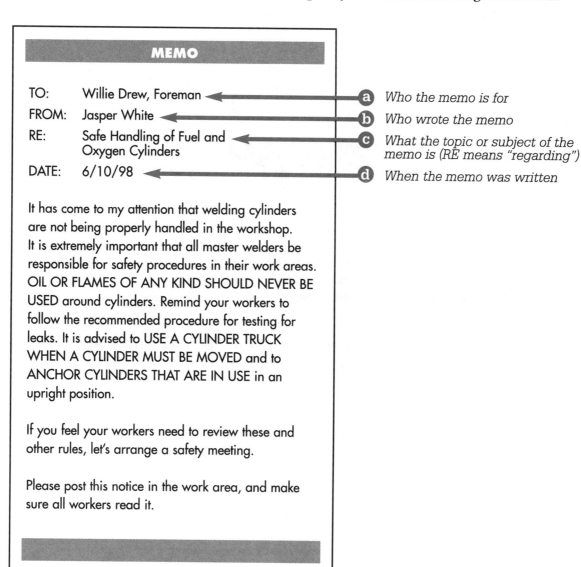

MEMO

TO: Willie Drew, Foreman   **a** *Who the memo is for*

FROM: Jasper White   **b** *Who wrote the memo*

RE: Safe Handling of Fuel and
        Oxygen Cylinders   **c** *What the topic or subject of the memo is (RE means "regarding")*

DATE: 6/10/98   **d** *When the memo was written*

It has come to my attention that welding cylinders are not being properly handled in the workshop. It is extremely important that all master welders be responsible for safety procedures in their work areas. OIL OR FLAMES OF ANY KIND SHOULD NEVER BE USED around cylinders. Remind your workers to follow the recommended procedure for testing for leaks. It is advised to USE A CYLINDER TRUCK WHEN A CYLINDER MUST BE MOVED and to ANCHOR CYLINDERS THAT ARE IN USE in an upright position.

If you feel your workers need to review these and other rules, let's arrange a safety meeting.

Please post this notice in the work area, and make sure all workers read it.

Using Main Ideas to Understand What You Read

The main idea is the most important point a writer is making in a memo, in a paragraph or section of a manual, or in some other piece of writing. Key details in the writing give facts, tell more about, or explain the main idea.

To find main ideas, readers usually:
- Read the title and any subheadings to determine the topic.
- Read the details and identify the idea that links them together.
- Ask themselves, "What do these key details tell me about the topic? What general point is the writer making?"

Read the substance abuse policy below. The main ideas of sections are shown in bold, and the key details are shown in *italics*. Taken together, they tell about the main idea of the entire policy.

SUBSTANCE ABUSE POLICY

1.1 Drew Construction seeks to ensure a safe workplace for all employees and to uphold the strictest standards in the industry. The abuse of drugs in the workplace reduces job efficiency and increases absenteeism and sick leave. It also jeopardizes the lives and safety of fellow employees and threatens our fine reputation for safety and quality in workmanship.

1.2 As part of our policy, **Drew Construction maintains a 100% drug- and alcohol-free workplace.** *No illegal drugs or alcoholic beverages are allowed* on any Drew Construction site. Also, *no employee is to show any evidence on the job of having abused this policy.*

1.3 To help enforce our policy, **Drew employees may be required to undergo drug testing.** You may be tested *during the pre-employment phase.* You may also be tested *upon any reasonable suspicion* by a manager or fellow worker. Testing also will be required *after an accident or "near" accident.*

1.4 **Violations of this policy include the following incidents:**
- *Reporting to work under the influence of drugs or alcohol*
- *Using, possessing, selling, transferring, or distributing illegal drugs or alcohol* at any Drew construction site or while wearing the Drew uniform
- *Testing positive on a drug test* (regardless of whether such drugs were taken during work hours or during nonwork time) or
- *Refusing to take a drug test*

Anyone who violates our substance abuse policy will be subject to disciplinary action and possible termination.

This graphic shows how the main ideas of each section form the key details that support the main idea of the substance abuse policy.

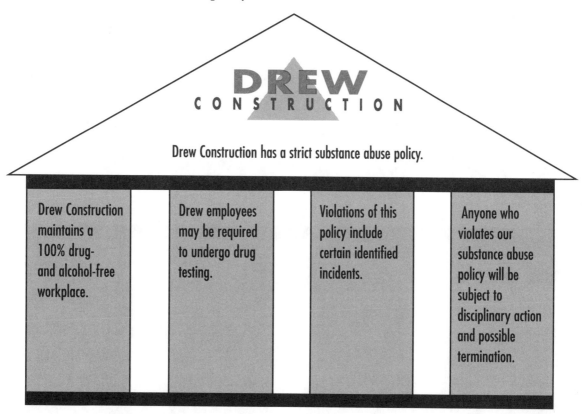

DREW
CONSTRUCTION

Drew Construction has a strict substance abuse policy.

| Drew Construction maintains a 100% drug- and alcohol-free workplace. | Drew employees may be required to undergo drug testing. | Violations of this policy include certain identified incidents. | Anyone who violates our substance abuse policy will be subject to disciplinary action and possible termination. |

For Your Own Use Here is a blank graphic organizer for you to copy. Use it to record the key details and main ideas of materials you must read on the job. Add more columns to support a main idea if you need to.

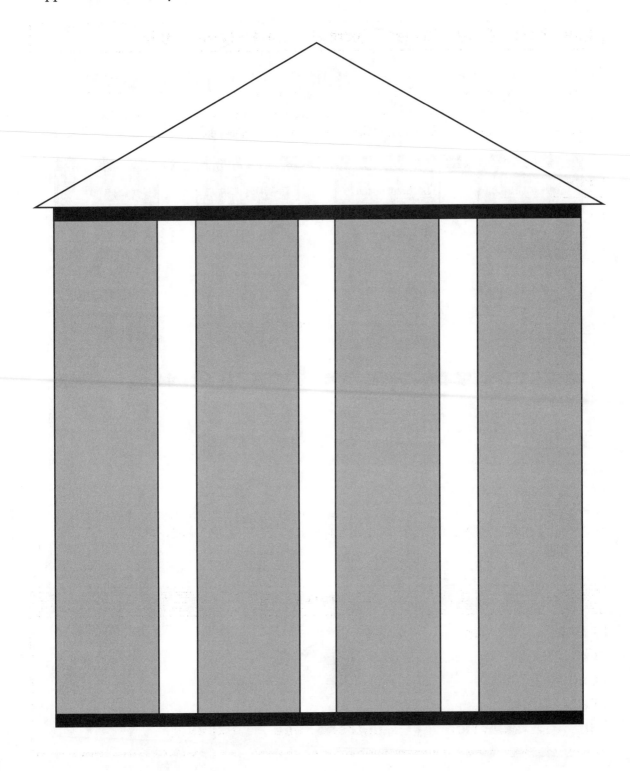

Using a Computer Menu

Many computer programs ask you to click on or highlight a main menu bar at the top of the screen. Many main menu bars look like this:

<u>F</u>ile   <u>E</u>dit   <u>V</u>iew   <u>I</u>nsert   <u>F</u>ormat   <u>T</u>ools   <u>T</u>able   <u>H</u>elp

Each of these commands in the main menu has its own menu of commands. To get to an internal menu, you can click on the whole word or hold the Alt key while typing the underlined letter key to open the menu. For example, if you clicked on File or used the Alt key and typed the letter *F*, you would then see a menu like this:

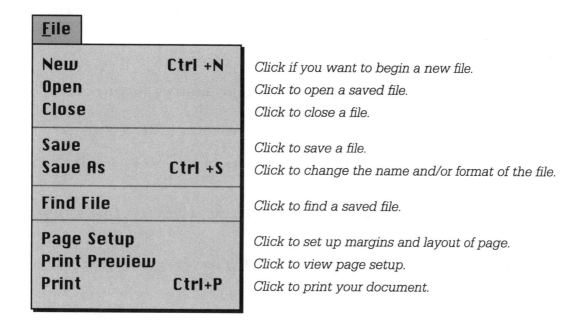

New Ctrl +N	*Click if you want to begin a new file.*
Open	*Click to open a saved file.*
Close	*Click to close a file.*
Save	*Click to save a file.*
Save As Ctrl +S	*Click to change the name and/or format of the file.*
Find File	*Click to find a saved file.*
Page Setup	*Click to set up margins and layout of page.*
Print Preview	*Click to view page setup.*
Print Ctrl+P	*Click to print your document.*

If you want to print a document you have just written, scan down to the final command—Print—and click on it. You will then see this screen of choices for printing a copy of your document:

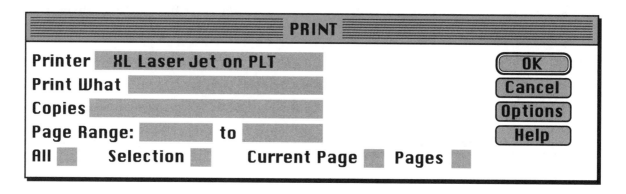

Using Context Clues

Context clues are words in the same sentence or in a nearby sentence that help you figure out the meaning of an unfamiliar word. A context clue can be:

- A definition of the word.
- An explanation or description.
- One or more examples.
- A synonym, or word similar in meaning.
- An antonym, or word opposite in meaning.
- The general sense of the sentence.

Read the sentences below. In each sentence is a context clue in *italics* that can help you figure out the meaning of the **bold** word or words. Before each sentence is the type of clue to look for.

The following context gives a definition:
The most important part of any technician's job is the ability to **diagnose,** *or figure out the cause of a problem.*

The following context gives an explanation, with descriptive details:
Laboratory conditions must be **sterile.** There can be *no trace of germs, dirt, or dust.*

The following context gives examples:
Put lower **denominations**—*ones, fives, and tens*—at the bottom of the stack of bills.

The following context uses a synonym of the word:
Personal days must have your supervisor's **authorization.** This *permission* must be in writing.

The following context uses an antonym of the word:
Use the **aerosol,** *not the liquid,* paint.

The general sense of the following context gives a clue:
Sick days do not **accrue.** *Any sick days that are not taken in one year are lost.*

Remember to look for context clues as you read to figure out the meanings of unfamiliar words. You can later check your guess by looking up each unfamiliar word in the dictionary.

Using the Dictionary

The word you look up in a dictionary is called an *entry* or *entry word.* A dictionary lists entry words in alphabetical order. If you are using a dictionary that does not have finger insets identifying where letters begin, here's a hint: Divide the dictionary into four imaginary sections: A through D, E through L, M through R, and S through Z. When you look up a word, turn to the section of the dictionary with the first letter of the word.

Finding the Word

Guide words are the words given at the upper left and upper right of each dictionary page. These words help you find, or guide you to, the entry word you are looking up. The guide words are usually in **bold** type. The one on the left is the first entry word on that dictionary page, and the one on the right is the last entry word.

Reading the Entry

Most dictionary entries consist of the following items:

*   **Entry word** in **bold** type. Entry words are usually given in syllables divided by bullets (•) or spaces.
*   **Pronunciation** of the word in parentheses or brackets. Most dictionaries use special symbols to show the sounds that the letters stand for. There is usually a key to these symbols on every other page.
*   **Parts of speech** and **variations in forms,** such as irregular plurals or verb forms.
*   **Definitions.** Most words have more than one meaning. The meanings are numbered.
*   **Sample sentences or phrases** to illustrate one or more of the meanings.
*   **Variations in spelling or forms.**

Below is a typical dictionary entry.

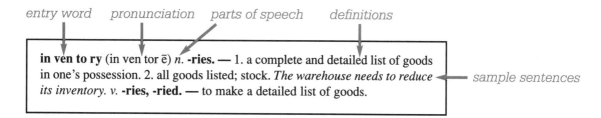

entry word   *pronunciation*   *parts of speech*   *definitions*

in ven to ry (in ven tor ē) *n.* **-ries.** — 1. a complete and detailed list of goods in one's possession. 2. all goods listed; stock. *The warehouse needs to reduce its inventory. v.* **-ries, -ried.** — to make a detailed list of goods.

sample sentences

Using a Chart to Organize Information

Below is a blank two-column chart. You can copy and use the chart as you read to organize different kinds of information—words and their definitions, measurements and their abbreviations, and so on.

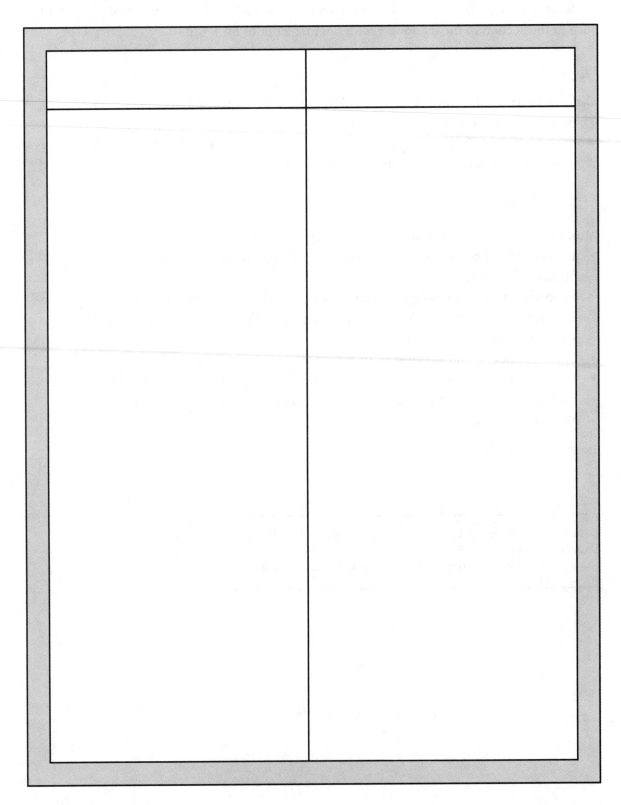

The Reading Process

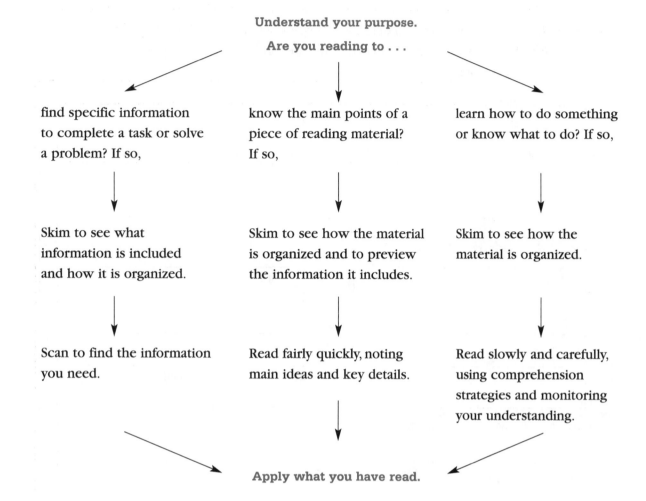

Understand your purpose.

Are you reading to . . .

find specific information to complete a task or solve a problem? If so,

know the main points of a piece of reading material? If so,

learn how to do something or know what to do? If so,

Skim to see what information is included and how it is organized.

Skim to see how the material is organized and to preview the information it includes.

Skim to see how the material is organized.

Scan to find the information you need.

Read fairly quickly, noting main ideas and key details.

Read slowly and carefully, using comprehension strategies and monitoring your understanding.

Apply what you have read.

Reading a Form

A form is a document with blank spaces in which specific information can be inserted. When you first see a form, skim it to determine its purpose and the kinds of information it asks for. Then read each line and area of the form carefully. If you are completing a form, always double-check your work.

Here is a computerized form that is used as an order form, a packing list placed inside a shipment, and an invoice for the goods that have been ordered and shipped.

The blank spaces are for inserting asked-for information. On a computer, these areas are called **fields.**

SHIPPING ORDER/PACKING LIST   **ELECTRONIC TOWN**

Sold To: Ship To:

Date Printed: Time Printed:

Order Number	Order Date	Salesperson	P.O. Number

Customer Number	Terms	Ship Via

Bin	Part #	Qty.	Description	Price	Total

This document is your invoice.

Subtotal _____
Shipping/Handling _____
Sales Tax _____
TOTAL _____

Reading a Chart or Schedule

A chart organizes information in rows and columns. Each heading tells you what kind of information is in that row or column.

A schedule is a special kind of chart. It tells workers the hours and days they must work or the dates by which certain things must be produced. Here is a sample work schedule for salespersons at Kentucky Motors car dealership.

To read the schedule, skim the information at the top of the chart. Then skim the days of the week across the top of the columns and the names at the beginning of the rows.

To find out a particular worker's hours on a certain day, scan down to find the worker's name, then across to the column under that day. Where the row and the column meet, you will find the information you are looking for.

INDIANA MOTORS SALESPERSON WORK SCHEDULE

Business Hours: Monday-Thursday 9:00 AM – 9:00 PM   Friday & Saturday 9:00—7:30

Name	MON	TUES	WED	THURS	FRI	SAT
Team A Phone Time 12:30 - 1:30 - Rotation every 3rd Week - 5:50 Saturdays						
Raymond	9 to 6	12 to 9	12 to 9	12 to 9	OFF	9 to 7:30
Nat	12 to 9	OFF	10 to 7	12 to 9	11 to 7:30	9 to 7:30
Valentina	12 to 9	9 to 6	OFF	12 to 9	11 to 7:30	9 to 7:30
Bob	9 to 6	12 to 9	12 to 9	12 to 9	OFF	9 to 7:30
Khalil	1 to 9	1 to 9	9 to 6	1 to 9	OFF	9 to 7:30
Team B Phone Time 1:30 - 2:30						
Charity	12 to 9	OFF	9 to 6	1 to 9	9 to 5:30	9 to 7:30
Kirk	9 to 6	12 to 9	OFF	1 to 9	11 to 7:30	9 to 7:30
Jack	9 to 6	OFF	12 to 9	12 to 9	11 to 7:30	9 to 7:30
Terry	1 to 9	12 to 9	OFF	12 to 9	11 to 7:30	9 to 7:30
Team C Phone Time 2:30 - 3:30						
Hasib	12 to 9	11 to 9	9 to 5	OFF	11 to 7:30	9 to 7:30
Maria	12 to 9	9 to 5	9 to 5	OFF	11 to 7:30	9 to 7:30
Igal	1 to 9	12 to 9	1 to 9	9 to 6	OFF	9 to 7:30
Bill	9 to 6	12 to 9	1 to 9	OFF	11 to 7:30	9 to 7:30
Note: All salespersons are scheduled at 9 AM on Saturday						

Managers	Team					
Celia	A	9 to 6	1 to 9	11 to 9	1 to 9	OFF	11 to 7:30
Andrew	B	12 to 9	OFF	12 to 9	1 to 9	9 to 5:30	9 to 5:30
Roy	C	1 to 9	12 to 9	12 to 9	OFF	12 to 7:30	9 to 7:30
Jorge	USED	11 to 9	11 to 9	OFF	9 to 9	10 to 7:30	10 to 7:30
Angela	NEW	11 to 8	11 to 8	11 to 8	OFF	11 to 8	9 to Close

Reading a Diagram

Diagrams are pictorial instructions. They are useful when you must learn how to do something or use something. First skim a diagram to see what it is explaining. Then read the text that goes with it, including labels, legends, and other key features.

Look at the diagram of a computer keyboard below. It has a picture of a typical keyboard with reference numbers to explain the purpose of certain keys.

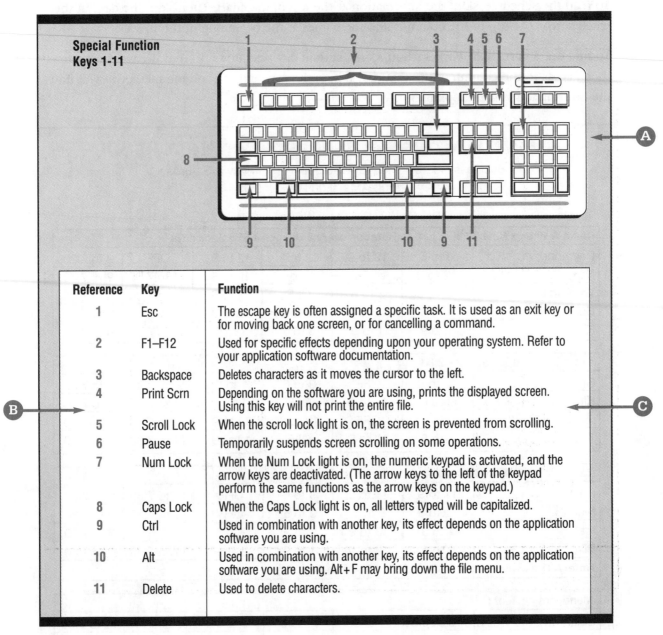

Reference	Key	Function
1	Esc	The escape key is often assigned a specific task. It is used as an exit key or for moving back one screen, or for cancelling a command.
2	F1–F12	Used for specific effects depending upon your operating system. Refer to your application software documentation.
3	Backspace	Deletes characters as it moves the cursor to the left.
4	Print Scrn	Depending on the software you are using, prints the displayed screen. Using this key will not print the entire file.
5	Scroll Lock	When the scroll lock light is on, the screen is prevented from scrolling.
6	Pause	Temporarily suspends screen scrolling on some operations.
7	Num Lock	When the Num Lock light is on, the numeric keypad is activated, and the arrow keys are deactivated. (The arrow keys to the left of the keypad perform the same functions as the arrow keys on the keypad.)
8	Caps Lock	When the Caps Lock light is on, all letters typed will be capitalized.
9	Ctrl	Used in combination with another key, its effect depends on the application software you are using.
10	Alt	Used in combination with another key, its effect depends on the application software you are using. Alt+F may bring down the file menu.
11	Delete	Used to delete characters.

(A) *Find the reference number for the key you are looking up. Use the lines on the picture that show the location of specific keys.*

(B) *Look up the key's reference number on the chart.*

(C) *Here you will find its name under Key and how you can use the key under Function.*

Reading a Flowchart

Flowcharts are pictorial instructions that show steps in a process. The steps are given in boxes or other shaped figures. The words *Yes* and *No* are judgments or decisions you must make along the way. Arrows show you the direction you need to go from one step to another, depending on your decision. By the end of the flowchart, you will have completed the instructions to a successful outcome.

For example, the flowchart below shows steps in the process of setting up a printer on a computer.

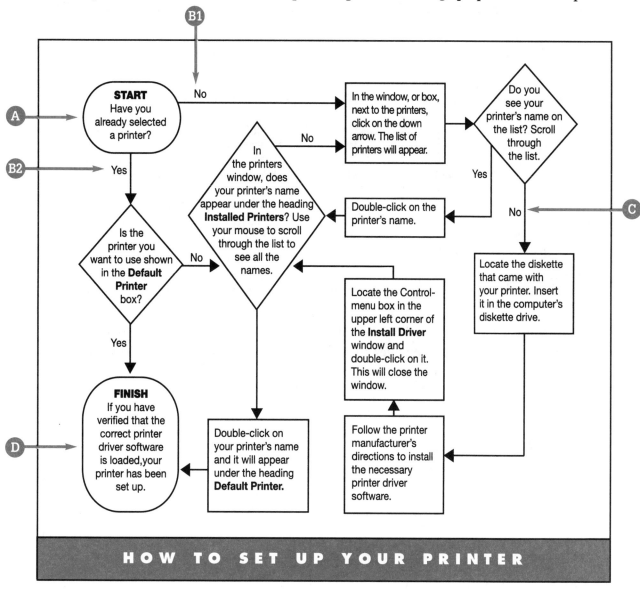

HOW TO SET UP YOUR PRINTER

A *Read and answer the first question.*

B1 *If your answer is no, follow this arrow to the next step.*

B2 *If your answer is yes, follow this arrow to the next step.*

C *Continue answering questions and following the appropriate arrows.*

D *The process is completed here.*

Using Parts of a Reference—Table of Contents and Index

Using a Table of Contents Skimming a table of contents is the best way to find out what a book contains. Main sections and sometimes subsections are listed in the order in which they appear in the book, along with the number of the page on which each begins. Below is a table of contents from a catering manual.

Table of Contents

Using an Index An index is at the very end of a book. It lists the topics covered in the book and the numbers of the pages on which they appear. The topics, or entries, are listed in alphabetical order. Here is part of an index from a catering manual.

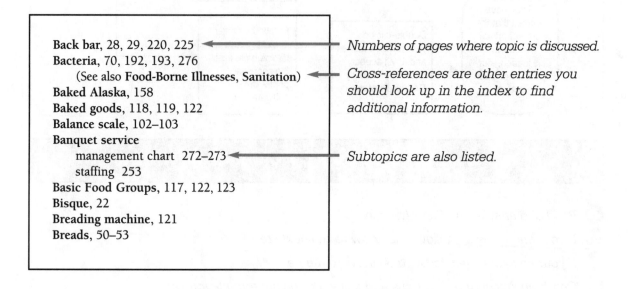

Numbers of pages where topic is discussed.

Cross-references are other entries you should look up in the index to find additional information.

Subtopics are also listed.